THE
SINGLE
JOURNEY

Discovering the Adventure of the Single Life

PETER M. NADEAU

The Single Journey by Peter Nadeau
Copyright 2005 by Peter M. Nadeau
All rights reserved.
ISBN: 1-59755-032-9

Published by: Advantage Books
                www.advbooks.com

This book and parts thereof may not be reproduced in any form, stored in a retrieval system or transmitted in any form by any means (electronic, mechanical, photocopy, recording or otherwise) without prior written permission of the publisher, except as provided by United States of America copyright law.

Unless otherwise noted, Scripture quotations are from the *Holy Bible*, **New Living Translation**, copyright 1996. Used by permission of Tyndale House Publishers, Inc., Wheaton, Illinois 60189. All rights reserved.

Scripture quotations noted ESV are from *The Holy Bible,* English Standard Version. Copyright 2001 by Crossway Bibles. All rights reserved.

Scripture quotations noted The Message are from *The Message: The New Testament in Contemporary English.* Copyright 1993 by Eugene H. Peterson.

Scripture quotations noted NIV are from *The Holy Bible: New International Version.* Copyright 1973, 1978, 1984 by International Bible Society. Used by permission of Zondervan Publishing House. All rights reserved.

Library of Congress Control Number: 2005926070

First Printing: May 2005

05 06 07 08 09 10 11   9 8 7 6 5 4 3 2 1
Printed in the United States of America

For Jilly,

ma sœur et mon amie

The Single Journey

TABLE OF CONTENTS

Acknowledgments 7

Introduction 11

Chapter One: Loneliness 15

Chapter Two: Identity 33

Chapter Three: Dreams 51

Chapter Four: Friends 69

Chapter Five: Mentors 89

Chapter Six: Dating 105

Chapter Seven: Sex 127

Chapter Eight: Hope 147

About the Author 165

The Single Journey

ACKNOWLEDGMENTS

SINGLE FRIENDS. Neal, Lenden, Shawn, Collin, Luke, Amy, Dawn, Heidi, Ethan, Jim, Shelly, Mitch, Ron, Dale, Kathy, Kerry, Laura, Megan, and Warner. All of you have shared your stories and wisdom with me and consequently improved this project. Thank you for looking past my faults and loving me.

MY FAITHFUL SUNDAY SCHOOL CLASS. Thanks so much for letting me explore new ideas and concepts with you each week. Your support, encouragement, and prayers carried me in the last year.

PRISCILLA. You continued to believe after I had given up on this project, and now look what God has done. I do not deserve such a wonderful fan as you. Thank you for your bold kindness.

LOUISE. You are the queen of hearts and I am wiser from spending time with you. Your passion for the gospel and compassion for the hearts of others is supernatural.

PAULA. Our meeting was ordained from above and I knew from our first conversation that God had given me a big sister. I would have lost the trail, and this book in the process, if you had not walked alongside me. You mean so much to me.

EILEEN. I am amazed at the gift God has given you. You were the perfect editor for this project. You edited the text, but did not eliminate me. God only has big plans for people to whom He gives such incredible gifts.

BRENT. You met me in the valley of the shadow of death and walked alongside me. Your wisdom is profound, your experience is invaluable, and your strength is like steel. Thank you for walking through the shadows with me. I love ya man.

LARRY. My captain, my partner, my teammate, my friend. You brought a boy into the wild and made him a man. You set the stage and invited me into my glory. You taught me the ways of the Force. You helped me find my cape. My heart skips a beat to sit at your feet. It is impossible to thank you for all you have done. I love you Wild.

DAD AND MOM. There has never been a time that you have not been there, loved me, or supported me. If I achieve anything in my life it will be because you loved me from the beginning. Everyone should have parents this great.

JILL. What do you say to someone who has loved you and made you laugh from the first day of their life? You have always been my best friend. We share the same blood and sometimes I think the same mind as well. I smile at the woman of God you have become. You inspired me in this project from the beginning and cheered for me along the way. It is dedicated to you because it would never have happened without you. Few siblings have what we have. I love you Jilly.

JESUS – You are my hero and my liberator. All praise to you for releasing me from my prison, giving me a new heart, and training my hands for war. Forgive me for doubting you when you were doing the most. Do a new work in your kingdom citizens who are single. The loneliness is too much without you. Thank you for reminding me that you know what it is like to be single.

The Single Journey

INTRODUCTION

Frodo did not get very far on his journey before he considered turning back. In the first film of *The Lord of the Rings* trilogy, the diminutive hobbit agreed to take possession of the legendary One Ring, and to see it destroyed in the fires of Mount Doom. To get there, he had to take a long journey over treacherous terrain and defeat the overwhelming armies arrayed against him. It was a grueling call. At every turn, I wondered whether it would be Frodo's last – when would he say, "Enough is enough!" and give up the quest? At one point, feeling completely dejected, Frodo confessed to his wizard friend, Gandalf, that he wished he had never started the journey in the first place. The wizard responded with some very wise words:

> FRODO: I wish the ring had never come to me. I wish none of this had happened.
>
> GANDALF: So do all who live to see such times. But that is not for them to decide. All we have to decide is what to do with the time that is given to us.

Many times I have felt like Frodo. I am still on the single journey even though it is not what I want. After many years of waiting, I still have not found a spouse with whom to spend the rest of my life. I am still fighting enemies all around me, and the end of my journey seems farther away than ever. When I chose to put marriage off after college, I figured the choice would always be there whenever I was ready. Prolonged singleness and marrying later in life seemed like a wise decision. Now sometimes I wish singleness had never come to me. I wish none of it had happened.

But counsel like Gandalf's sharpens my perspective. The truth picks me up and brushes me off so that I can take another step. No one walks this earth feeling perfectly content with life. Everyone wishes they could change something about their circumstances. The unemployed want a job. The sick long to be well. The barren desire a child. Singles plead with God for a mate. Clearly we all have times of struggle. The question is, what we will do with the time that is given to us?

I did not expect my life to turn out this way. I assumed I would be like everyone else. After all, doesn't everyone get married by the time they are twenty-five? Certainly only the odd balls are still single after that age. Right? It turns out that I am one of the odd balls. I did not know when I left college I was setting out on the single journey. Not until my late twenties did I realize that I had still not found a lifetime companion and I was not happy about it. As a result I have had to learn how to traverse the unique landscape of the single journey. I have befriended many fellow travelers along the way. I have learned to identify the particular enemies that lurk in the forests of this quest. Gradually I have come to learn who I am and where I am going. Most importantly I have learned never to give up and never to turn back.

This book was not written to help you find Mr. or Mrs. Right. It is not a guide for dating, a strategy to find a mate, or a list of tips for snaring the guy or girl of your dreams. It is not a message to "suck it up" and pretend you do not care about being single and alone. Neither is it an order to get busy in the church - singles get plenty of that stuff in a host of other places, whether they want it or not.

This book was written to acknowledge the pain of loneliness and disappointment; to give you a great hope for the future; and to help you discover the potential for living an abundant life as long as you are single. It is a validation of your loneliness, an invitation to live, and liberation from unbelief. It is a voice - the voice of a fellow traveler calling for singles to enlarge their desires and surrender their control. It is an encouragement to live a kingdom identity rather than a single identity. It is a dream. A dream from a fellow traveler that God's single men and women will come alive like never before and reflect the glory of their Sovereign.

These pages are not my biography, however, I have tried to include many personal stories to help you remember I am on the path with you. I will try to share some of the wisdom given to me over the years. In the meantime, let us bare each other's burdens and permit ourselves to admit we are lonely and longing for love. Let us explore these paths to the fullest measure. Let us walk in strength, slay our enemies, and enjoy the view. Finally let us live freely and abundantly with the time that has been given to us.

The Single Journey

CHAPTER ONE

LONELINESS

The body is a house of many windows; there we all sit, showing ourselves and crying on the passers-by to come and love us.
— Robert Louis Stevenson

When the heart of man shuts out, Sometimes the heart of God takes in, And fences them all round about, With silence mid the world's loud din.
— James Russell Lowell

You know what I long for, Lord; you hear my every sigh.
— (Ps. 38:9)

    I went to the Florida Keys for the first time when I was five years old. I have few memories of this visit except for the intense heat and an infamous strawberry ice cream cone. The 97 degree temperature melted my sweet treat faster than I could eat it and soon a pink mush dribbled down the cone onto my hand. For the rest of the day I was wiping my forehead with pink, sticky fingers.

Despite this early childhood misfortune I keep returning to the Keys. My more recent fascination with the islands began four years ago when I helped chaperone a group of students to Big Pine Key for a science fieldtrip. We learned about plankton, different types of mangrove trees, and which sharks are dangerous and which are not. Night-wading for trumpet fish and snorkeling at Bahia Honda State Park convinced me that I had found my personal paradise.

Many times since that trip with my students I have returned to my paradise, sometimes for a dive trip, other times to be by myself to think and listen to God. Something about these islands thrills me – thousands of patches of land, big and small, scattered at the base of the Florida peninsula to form a fishhook, surrounded by an aqua sea, and connected by bridge after bridge. The Keys are my favorite place to get away.

For centuries Floridians have found a variety of treasure in these islands. The early Indian inhabitants valued the islands for the fish and turtles they could pull from the sea. For many years pirates preyed on unsuspecting travelers and ships that ran aground on the long and shallow shelf surrounding the Keys. Henry Flagler, who made millions from building hotels throughout Florida, hoped to bring tourists to the Keys by constructing an overseas rail line linking Key West with the mainland. The project, completed in 1912, was badly damaged by a massive hurricane in 1935. After World War II when pink gold (shrimp) was discovered as a lucrative treasure, the islands experienced steady growth in population. Now thousands of tourists, like me, travel each year to the Florida Keys and discover the treasures of diving, fishing, kayaking, or simply the golden sunshine.

Chapter One – Loneliness

At sunset I settle down on the rocks of Sombrero Beach. My shorts are slightly damp from this morning's dive. My stomach is filled with a blackened grouper that was probably swimming this morning. I begin to sketch the drama that unfolds each evening here. A small fishing boat motors into the lagoon, sailboats haul in their sails at the dock, and the orange sun slips below the horizon turning the palm trees into silhouettes against a fiery sky. Slowly the orange ball in the distance draws closer to the dark blue of the sea. I count the seconds until it disappears. *Four... three...two...one... touchdown!*

It is perfect once again - a scene of unmatched serenity and beauty. I capture it all on my sketchpad, but then I hesitate. I stop and put the pad down. The feeling has returned even amidst this perfection. The location is exotic and captivating. The feelings are powerful and the scene is complete - except for one thing. I am alone, again.

THE HUNGER WITHIN

At times I have felt so desperately lonely that I have wanted to make a "Wilson" just to have somebody to talk to. Wilson, if you do not remember, was the name of a volleyball that became Tom Hank's best friend while stranded alone on an island in the movie *Castaway*. Though Wilson was inanimate and inarticulate, Tom Hanks still needed somebody to talk to, so he chose a volleyball. I can sympathize with him.

If there is an organ in the body that causes loneliness I am sure it is located near the stomach. When I am lonely I feel a deep hunger inside, as if I have been hollowed out and something has been taken away. When I am *really* hungry I will eat anything, even if it is not my favorite kind of food. As a fussy eater I am not quite so fussy when I am starved. Lettuce, ice, dried pasta, or frozen peas – anything will do if I am hungry enough. The same is true when I am lonely. I will look anywhere or do anything to stop the hunger.

I know I am lonely when I check my email, click on another site, and then check my box again to see if mail came in. *Maybe I missed something.* Sometimes I will dial the voicemail on my cell phone to check for messages, even though the very colorful, highly detailed, and very accurate display screen says, "no new messages." *Maybe the screen messed up.* When I pull into my driveway I bound out of the front seat and eagerly run to my mailbox only to find bills, coupon packets, and ads for credit cards. *Why would anyone send me a letter?* There is one more chance. I plow through the front door with my hands full, dropping things in the entrance way, and dash to my office to check my home phone. *Aha!* The little green light on my caller ID box is flashing. *A new message!* I dial into the system. I punch in my code. I wait. I frown. I hang up. *Another telemarketer wants to sell me solar heating for my pool.*

Now as that unidentified organ near my stomach begins to pump the lonely feeling into my body from ears to toes, I resort to the backup plan. Noise, motion, a task, or any distraction is all I need to stave off the growing hunger. I turn on the radio. *Nuts! Commercials.* I turn on the TV. *Fifty-five channels of boredom.* I eat. *I just bought these cookies how can they be stale?* I drink. *Remember to buy more milk.* I sleep. *Why do all my neighbors have dogs?* I do laundry. I mow the lawn. I write out bills. I make my bed. I play video games. I write. I run errands. I organize my closet. I read. I vacuum. I desperately search for any distraction to deaden the pain.

Until I find myself sitting on my couch and thinking. *Maybe I should call somebody. I haven't talked to Dave in a while.* Dave moved to Colorado three years ago and since then we have talked twice. *What about Brandy in New Jersey? We need to catch up.* I have not talked to Brandy at all in two years. If someone does call to ask a quick question, I become unusually friendly. *So how are you? What's new with you? So good to hear from you.* I am sure the caller on the other end can see through my charade.

Now the organ inside is working overtime. I am consumed with loneliness. I am empty inside. I grow bitter. *Why don't more people call me? I'm a nice guy.* I think about all the things I have done for other people and wonder why they do not do more for me. I think about Friday night approaching and I have received no invitations and made no plans. Time for a one-man pity party. *I bet everybody is going out on Friday night except me.* I embellish the fantasy in my mind by imagining all my friends at a rocking party with great music in the background. They are all standing around with beautiful partners on their arms.

Why is everybody happy and connected except me? I shouldn't have to live like this. I am made for so much more.

Indeed I am.

AT LAST!

I am sure that if a survey was taken, the most often quoted Bible verse among singles would be Genesis 2:18 in which God declares, "It is not good for man to be alone." I have personally browbeaten God with this verse many times, but with few results. God, Himself, said it is not good for a man to be alone. I figure sometimes I need to remind Him of that fact.

We can all understand Adam's predicament. Imagine yourself in a perfect world, a world where you get to design everything according to your specifications. What would it be like? A tropical paradise? An alpine getaway? A secluded cabin in the woods? How would you spend your time? Golfing? Skiing? Painting? Writing? The weather is always perfect in your world, you never get sick, and you have enough money and time to do whatever you want, whenever you want. Put the book down for a moment and try to imagine what your perfect world would look like.

Now I am going to make one qualification. You get to be anywhere, do anything, and have as much as you want except for one thing – you are alone. You are the only one there to enjoy your perfect world. There is no one else. Do you want it now? I didn't think so. There is something about our nature that desires, and even requires, contact and connection with other people.

Adam's story is not much different from that of many singles. He strikes out into the world ready to prove he can survive in the jungle. Due to lack of competition he builds a very successful landscaping business that dominates the market and he is careful to avoid the riskier sections of town. Yet, when Adam does take time to smell the roses, he too feels the hunger of loneliness. Alarmed by the realization that success is not enough, he longs for somebody special in his life; somebody who can help with the business and comfort him when he comes home at night.

So he hits the local singles scene in hopes of finding a life partner. He's not a real sharp dresser, but he's confident his perfect body and perfect character will suffice. Night after night he checks out the action, but everybody has their own exclusive clique. He meets some great chicks, cats, and foxes, but nobody who can truly understand him. Heartbroken he storms out of the club, calling everyone names as he leaves, and goes home to bed early.

Then comes the part that we all long for as singles. While Adam sleeps, he dreams of meeting a perfect mate. This mate is a lot like him and they have much in common, but there is also something very different. The mate can do things he cannot do, understand things in ways he cannot understand, and most of all complete whatever is lacking in himself. Together their life is fulfilling and really, really good.

Adam awakes and a sharp pain in his side makes him think the night before was a lot rougher than he remembers. Then he realizes he is not imagining or dreaming. Like a slow motion scene in a music video she appears - the most captivating and enticing creature he has ever seen! At once he knows she compliments him perfectly. She is his type. Boy, is she his type! She is just like him, yet she is different - different in all the right places and in all the right ways. Like Adam, she is not much of a dresser, but that's just fine with him. He stands there in a trance for several moments. He is speechless – stunned - awed. And then he utters those famous words, "Woe Man!" The name stuck. Adam then composed the first love song called "At Last!"

> *This at last is bone of my bones*
> *and flesh of my flesh;*
> *she shall be called Woman,*
> *because she was taken out of Man.*
>
> — (Gen. 2:23; ESV)

The song skyrockets to the top of the charts. It is played in all the local clubs and everyone else on the prowl is envious of this pair. They are the pinnacle of creation, the best blind date ever, and the first celebrity couple.

Adam's sense of loneliness before the creation of Eve was not just some silly feeling. The image bearer of God truly was incomplete for his task without his partner. God, Himself, declared Adam's isolation "not good." Together Adam and Eve are perfect strength and perfect beauty. They are one. They are complete. Apart from each other there is a sense of disjointedness.

These verses can be painful for singles. We can almost finish the sentence before we read it on the page because we know firsthand the experience of being alone and disconnected. We long for Adam and Eve's scene to be our scene. We are moved by powerful and romantic encounters in movies because we want the same in our lives. We pray for the perfect companion, chosen by God, who is the right match in every way. Both men and women are created in the image of God, whether they are separate or together, yet each often feel incomplete until becoming one flesh with a spouse. Friends and family try to comfort us, but as long as we are single there is a good chance that we will continue to feel that something is missing. This is natural. Regardless of how many friends we have, loneliness will still be a struggle.

That is why Genesis 2:18 can encourage us. It validates our sense of drifting and apartness. There is not something wrong with us. This verse not only tells us we will feel lonely and alone, but something is wrong if we do not.

I know too many singles who pretend they are not lonely and pretend they do not care about marriage. At times, I fight that same temptation. It is easier to deny the angst of being without a soul mate than to step into the abyss of loneliness. Stifling a desire makes us feel in control. Acknowledging a desire makes us vulnerable, yet a desire that is not open is a desire that cannot be filled. The singleness of Adam reminds all singles that loneliness is normal and necessary.

This is affirming to me because often I grow weary of the single life. I want to throw in the towel because everything seems out of place in my life. I took a wrong turn somewhere back there; nothing is going right. I need a new job. I need to change churches. I need new hobbies. I need new friends. I need to move to a new city. Yet when I calm down and take a good look at my life, I realize I actually like my life. I like my job. I like my church. I enjoy my hobbies. I value my friends. I love where I live. I am just out of sorts because I feel unconnected. But it's okay, I should. Adam had the same feeling until God gave him Eve. Until the day that I am united with my Eve then I, too, will feel out of sorts. I am made for so much more. Loneliness is the whaling siren that does not let me forget.

YOU SHOULD GET MARRIED

Friends and family do not let us forget it either. In the midst of our struggle with loneliness we seem to be barraged by well-meaning folks trying to offer a quick fix for our problems. I have to chuckle when somebody says to me, "Well, if you're lonely why don't you just get married?" I feel like saying, "Gee, thanks. The thought never occurred to me. I'll put that on tomorrow's To-Do list."

The prevailing message given to and believed by many singles is that marriage is the goal of life. Celibacy was the pinnacle of one's spirituality in the Middle Ages. Today marriage has replaced it. Indeed the church has reinforced this message. Often singles feel patronized by the married 30+ crowd who are raising families and look upon singles in bewilderment. "You obviously messed up somewhere along the way. Your life should be more like mine," they say, as they yell at their toddler and complain about their spouse.

Often singles feel shuffled around in a church and are the last group to receive attention; yet singles are usually the ones with the most free time and disposable income in the church. Nevertheless, singles in the church are often given the choice of feeling like a third wheel around married folks or joining *youth group redivivus*, also known as a singles group. This is the place where you meet a lot of people who you know why they are still single, so you hop on the first dating train that comes to get out of town.

And then the frightful day comes when you open your mail to find a wedding invitation from your best friend. Ever since they started dating you have seen precious little of them. (They took the last train out remember.) But you know it will be rude if you do not go, so you put your best foot forward, wear your favorite outfit, and give yourself plenty of pep talks about it being your turn someday, and you manage to get yourself to the wedding with a strained smile. You do not find your seat before three different people ask you if you are dating someone. *Umm, no not right now,* you mumble. You survive the ceremony, but as you are throwing confetti at the newlyweds, other guests are throwing darts at you.

"What about her? She's nice."

"You can't wait forever."

Chapter One – Loneliness

"You're not getting any younger."

"Don't you want to get married?"

"Do you have commitment issues?"

Your favorite obscenities are on the tip of your tongue, but you need to keep a good face at the reception. The meal is not bad and although you have been assigned to the same table as all the other lonely hearts, you manage to have one or two decent conversations. But then the moment of horror arrives. A way too suave DJ with a 70s suit and a game show host haircut requests all the unmarried guys and girls to come to the dance floor. You cringe. You forgot about this part.

The groom is about to toss the garter to the guys and the bride will toss her bouquet to the girls. Those who catch it will be predestined to walk the aisle. You knew it was coming and had planned to be in the restroom at this moment, but you lost track of time. The older folks are nudging you to the dance floor. You think in vain for an excuse to escape. You consider swallowing your ice water in one gulp. If you are choking then they cannot make you do this. But it is too late. You are already there. You stand there with the other "un's", unmotivated, underachievers, unmarrieds, like cattle at a beef auction. Suddenly you see the garter or bouquet flying in your direction. You scurry the other way. The others play rugby for a few moments on the floor as you stand to the side with an "aw shucks, I missed" look. Finally, one happy soul emerges with the coveted prize and you walk briskly back to your seat. Ah, there it is, your integrity. You knew you left it somewhere.

LONELINESS - WHAT IS IT GOOD FOR?

Of course it is not quite this bad all the time, but between the powerful feelings of loneliness within us and the hailstorm of pressure from others, it is very tempting to stifle our God-given desires for intimacy, romance, and union because they are just too painful. Holding onto the desire for intimacy in this world is like trying to hold a dozen eggs in one hand. It does not take much for us to give up and call ourselves foolish. It is, therefore, no wonder that most singles are reluctant to open up about their deep loneliness, even with other singles. They are more accustomed to misunderstanding and misguided attempts to "fix" their condition than they are to receiving genuine sympathy and compassion.

So what do many singles do when they are intensely lonely and bombarded with disheartening messages? They do what is logical. They do what they are told. They get married; if not to another lonely single, then to their job, their hobby, their ministry, or anything else that will kill the hunger of loneliness. "I know I hide behind being busy with my job," a single told me recently. "But it's just easier that way."

Ironically what many singles need is not a marriage, but rather a divorce - a divorce from the idolatrous relationships they have formed to kill their hunger pangs of loneliness. In truth, our desire for union with another cannot be met unless that desire is acknowledged, enlarged, and available. Often God cannot put good things in our hands because they are already too full with idols. Detours around loneliness are such idols.

If most of us had the choice we would marry as soon as possible; we would do anything to get rid of the "disease" of our singleness. I have begged, bargained, screamed, yelled, cried, and pleaded with God, yet, He has not budged. At times I doubted He even cared until He would come to me gently and speak – reminding me of His goodness and His love for me.

So why should we smash the idols and look our loneliness in the eye? Because God wants to do more, say more, and change far more in us than just our marital status. He wants to use our loneliness in a profound way. Singles have an awesome window of time in their lives to discover who they are in God's great story and where they are headed. We need to cherish the freedom to listen to God's voice without the hindrances of a demanding spouse, a wailing toddler, or a ludicrous schedule. Loneliness can be one of God's greatest gifts to singles.

When someone first told me to treasure this time in my life and embrace my loneliness as a gift from God, I thought they were crazy. *How insensitive can you get? Don't you know I would do anything to get rid of this gnawing inside?* Yet, gradually, I have come to appreciate the wisdom behind those words.

AN UNEXPECTED GIFT

Loneliness is a gift from God because it is a continual reminder that I am created for so much more. Not just union with a spouse, but also a deeper connection with my family and friends, and most of all intimacy with my Creator. Loneliness pushes me forward when I would be otherwise tempted to settle for lackluster relationships and an isolated existence.

The temptation is within all of us to retreat when we are disappointed or hurt by others. We want to pull up the drawbridge leading to our hearts. Loneliness beckons us to release that kind of control and to engage and connect with others. It is a reminder that we are fueled by relationships and that our tank is empty.

Sometimes, when loneliness gets the best of me, I become angry and bitter against God. How could He let this happen to me? I conclude He is cruel because He could give me a spouse in a flash and yet He refuses. So I choose to avoid Him and just go through the motions of religion. I mutter under my breath in disgust. But then, aware of my need, I fall before Him pleading and He always answers with comfort, hope, or new paths for the future. Without loneliness I would run from Him and not look back. However, I cannot because this creature was created for intimacy with its Creator.

Loneliness is also an opportunity. It is an opportunity for us to ask God what He wants to let surface in our hearts. It gets our attention and consequently we are driven to ask our Father what He is trying to tell us. *What are you trying to get me to notice Lord? What relational pattern are you trying to free me from? How am I sabotaging the good things you are trying to give me? Would marriage be destructive for me right now? What new thing do you want to do at this point in my journey?*

As much as I do not want to admit it, God has used my loneliness from time to time to convict me of sin. He has shown me *my* bitterness when I have blamed someone else. He has shown me *my* fear when I have claimed, "They're not my type." And He has also used my loneliness to propel me towards action. I have often found the motivation to hit the dance floor, to ask for a phone number, or to go new places because I was so tired of feeling alone.

Loneliness can also be a gift in marriage. Someday when I am married, after the initial fireworks of being a newlywed has worn off and I find myself feeling alone or bored, I hope that loneliness prompts me to connect even further with my mate. I hope loneliness compels me to seek more intimacy, greater understanding, and a deeper appreciation of the life partner God has given me. I pray now that I will resist the temptation then to seek connection with another woman. Trading in one spouse for another does not cure loneliness - it feeds it.

A friend asked me recently, "How do you like being a writer?" I thought and responded, "I love it. It's a great life, but…" Before I could finish he completed my sentence. "But it's a lonely life." He totally got it. He understood me and articulated what I was feeling. It was a relief to have somebody validate my feelings: I can enjoy my work, yet still feel lonely. It's quite normal for a writer to feel this way.

I say the same to singles. It is okay for you to feel lonely. Not only is it okay, but it is normal, natural, necessary, and healthy. In fact, something might be wrong if you do not, at times, feel like you are going to split in half from the ache. From the beginning God realized Adam needed a mate with whom to become one flesh. Unless you have deliberately chosen the single life in order to advance God's kingdom, then the same will be true for you. As long as that special someone is missing in your life, you will feel disjointed, unconnected, and only half of something. It is there that God most frequently opens His workshop in the heart of a single. The remodeling may be long and hard, but the dwelling is far better when the master carpenter is done.

Finally, loneliness brings me to a place of submission and surrender. The weight of a lonely heart is too great of a burden for me to bear. I struggle, strain, and grit my teeth to carry the load, but it becomes too much. I am forced to lay it at the feet of my Lord and let Him carry it. Surrendering our desires for intimacy to God is not the same as stifling those desires. When we surrender our desires for romance to Christ, we are admitting we are not in control of this area of our lives and neither do we want to be. We will heed His call to patience. We will wait for His best. When we kneel before our Father with uplifted hands, we have His promise that when we ask for bread He will not give us a stone.

THE LONELINESS OF JESUS

I am amazed at Jesus' example during the last night He spent with His disciples. Just hours away from the most grueling, brutal suffering that the Roman world offered, He knew full well what lay ahead. The Evil One was tempting Him away from the cross at every moment. When I am facing a great trial, I need loving and supportive friends around me. I believe Christ needed the same that night. In fact, He told His disciples that He had yearned for some time to share the supper with them. That meal has become known as the Last Supper; it was the last meal Jesus would share with His closest friends. The end had come. There would be no more exorcisms or mass feedings for now. The hour had finally arrived. Jesus' predictions regarding His death were about to come true. The horror of the Passion was about to begin.

Yet notice Jesus' primary concern. He is intent on drawing His disciples closer. As they argue over who will be the greatest in the Kingdom, He washes their feet. As they promise to stick by Him, He promises not to leave them without a Comforter. When Jesus retreats to the mountains to pray, He does not go alone. Rather He takes Peter, James, and John and repeatedly asks them to pray with Him in the Garden. The Son of God seeks the intimacy and encouragement of those He came to save at the most crucial hour in mankind's history. The next day He would be executed for them. That night He just wanted to be close to them.

I do not believe Jesus ever felt so alone during His earthly ministry as He did that night with His disciples. None of them understood what was about to happen. How could they? Instead they asked irrelevant questions and jockeyed for position. Still, Jesus sought to serve them, to encourage them, and to love them. He turned His deep feelings of loneliness into an opportunity to submit to His Father and connect with His friends. There is no better example for singles struggling with loneliness.

The Single Journey

CHAPTER TWO

IDENTITY

To be nobody but myself in a world which is doing its best, night and day, to make you everybody else – means to fight the hardest battle which any human being can fight, and never stop fighting.
-E.E. Cummings

I became my own only when I gave myself to Another.
- C.S. Lewis

If you try to keep your life for yourself, you will lose it. But if you give up your life for me, you will find true life.
- (Luke 9:24)

    I worked for several years as a history teacher in a local high school. It was my first real professional job after college and I looked forward to it with great anticipation. But when I told people what I did for a living, I would hear, "Gee, I'm sorry. That must be hard." Of course they were not referring to the history or the teaching. They were amazed that someone who was not an asylum escapee would actually be willing to work with teenagers all day. "I enjoy it," I would respond. "The kids are a lot of fun."

And indeed they were. Despite hours of obnoxious adolescent conversations, cleaning tons of toilet paper off of my house, and scraping giant wads of gum off of desks, I genuinely loved and enjoyed the teens I taught each day. *Alright, most of them anyway. They were great... Well, that is, some of them... Then again maybe I liked only the ones that liked me.*

Some of my best conversations with my students revolved around discussing the latest teen film. You know the type - movies that are set in a typical high school with all the usual characters. The quarterback of the football team is always strikingly handsome, but seems to live in his jersey. He is usually dating the captain of the cheerleading squad, who is ready to burst out of her skin with sunshine and cheeriness. The aggregate sum of their intelligence is slightly below that of a gecko. The computer nerds timidly creep across campus away from the jocks so that they can advance some dangerous technological plan in the lab that threatens the extinction of all mankind. The bookworms do three times the required homework, constantly adjust their oversized glasses, and secretly fantasize about the quarterback's girlfriend. Throw in a few surfer dudes, wallflower girls, grunge gurus, clueless teachers, and a neurotic principal, and you have all the necessary ingredients for another stock teen flick. Even a low budget and predictable screenwriting cannot prevent these movies from bringing in respectable box office sales.

My students could rattle off the typical characters in a teen movie faster than I could. They knew what to expect from the movie before the opening credits rolled. This world, albeit slightly exaggerated, was their world, their worries, and their people. Somewhere in that landscape of faces and identities they could find themselves, or a character with whom they could identify. Perhaps they could not quickly put it to words, but they knew who they most resembled and who, deep down, they wanted to be.

I would ask them, "How about it guys? Who are you? Which character have you chosen to be?" The class would grow quiet; they would look at me with a profound intensity, but I knew they were searching deep inside to see themselves. The silence would be deafening until some brave soul would come out of hiding. "I play the tough guy." He had to because he was shorter than all the other guys. "I play the teacher's pet," a girl would confess because she wanted adults to like her. "I am the jock," and everyone knew it was because he was good at soccer and poor at academics.

All my students had carefully crafted a smaller identity so that they could be noticed, accepted, congratulated, or gain control of an otherwise out of control situation. The promiscuous girls received respect from the shy girls. The bad boys felt a sense of power when they saw the fear in the eyes of the nice boys. The junior scholars thrived knowing they were at the top of the class; they were buoyant when a teacher would imply all the other students should be more like them. Suddenly a large portion of their lives made sense to them. They realized, in their own way, that they had surrendered large portions of life so that they could live a limited identity.

I had to laugh to myself when I had a whole room of teenagers looking at themselves so deeply, but I would also tell them that they were not alone. Their parents, their teachers, and, in fact, all adults do the same thing. It is just that we get better at it as we get older. Singles are no exception.

IDENTITY CRISIS

If you think about it, Jesus asked people to do something quite radical. He challenged a variety of people, many of whom were quite comfortable with their lives, to leave everything behind and follow Him.

> *Then he called his disciples and the crowds to come over and listen. 'If any of you wants to be my follower,' he told them, 'you must put aside your selfish ambition, shoulder your cross, and follow me. If you try to keep your life for yourself, you will lose it. But if you give up your life for my sake and for the sake of the Good News, you will find true life.*
> - (Mark 8:34-35)

That's quite a heavy mandate. Jesus gives few specifics about what the journey will look like down the road. All He says is put aside everything and follow Him. Were any of the disciples single? Probably so, and they most likely wondered how following Jesus would impact their marriage prospects. Nevertheless, they were too drawn to Jesus to turn away. Each of them, in their own way, turned from one identity to assume another. Matthew Levi gave up his identity as a tax collector. Peter gave up his identity as a fisherman. They all agreed to become new people with new identities.

Jesus' call on our lives is the same today. We are told to surrender all other identities and to live a new identity as a follower of Jesus Christ. All our agendas, schedules, and demands are to yield to this radical call of Christ on our lives. It is no longer our job to design our lives or present a facade that works well in the world. Our sense of self must be tied to the person of Christ. We receive our identity from Him.

Most singles, who are believers, are quite aware of these truths. Many of us strive to surrender our lives to Jesus every day. We long to follow Him. Yet to be honest, it often seems like Jesus does not deliver on His promise of true life, especially when we live sold out for Him. In fact, the more we try to do what's right, the more we seem to miss out. Finding our identities as followers of Jesus can be a pretty tall order and may seem inadequate for this world. We may desire Jesus to be the Lord of our life, but at times it seems He is not doing such a great job. Occasionally it feels like somebody hit the autopilot button and slipped out of the cabin.

For singles, their frustrated desire for marriage is the most obvious area that God seems to be absent. When my friend, Ann, was in college she prayed about her desire for a husband and told God, "You pick." Today she is 34 with no potential mate in sight. She did not forget to follow Jesus, but did Jesus forget her prayers?

When God does not seem to be doing a good job with our lives, we often decide to hop into the cockpit and take the controls for ourselves. Surely we could do a better job. After all, God has so many people on His mind perhaps we're not His top priority. Maybe He needs a little help with His busy schedule. And as far as finding our identity in following Jesus, that just doesn't seem to be working. Perhaps we need to come up with something a little more focused on getting us married. Thus singles try something they already tried in high school.

HARD TIMES AT SINGLES HIGH

Often the only difference between a local high school and a local singles group is that in a singles group there is no guarantee of getting out in four years. Since finding their identity as a follower of Christ has not worked out well, they adopt an identity reminiscent of that in high school, but this version is older and wiser and better suited for the local church's singles scene. The typical evening meeting goes something like this.

You arrive a few minutes early. This is perfect timing because you will be able to pick a strategic location, somewhere between your friends and where the new people sit. You must be available to talk to any potentials. That is, of course, why you are here. Unfortunately for you everyone else came early tonight and already grabbed the best seats. Now you will be forced to sit in the front with "Marry-Me Molly."

Molly is a sweet girl with a perpetual smile. She has already been here for half an hour, hoping to meet her future husband tonight. Then he will ask her out for the weekend, which is four days away, and on the sixteenth of the month. They will quickly begin dating, which will last five or six months. Next he will ask her to marry him on the anniversary of their first date, which would again be the sixteenth of the month. Their engagement will last for three months, maybe four if the country club is booked. Of course their wedding will be on the sixteenth of that month. Her dress will be the third one from the left, in the window of the cute little bridal shop on Gordon Street. Her man's tux will be jet black, with a white cummerbund and tails (the tails are a must). The wedding cake will be white chocolate, the honeymoon will be at her favorite bed and breakfast in Asheville, North Carolina, and together they will have three children, two girls and one boy, all two years apart and each born on the sixteenth of their respective birth months. Any other minor details she will leave to providence.

Chapter Two – Identity

Molly is a nice enough person, but she wears an invisible sign that says, "Marry me please!" You were able to figure that out on your own, but if you were not able to then "Counselor Carrie" or "Bitter Betty" would have told you. Carrie went back to school for her degree in counseling. No one would doubt her strong interpersonal skills, but strangely she has everyone figured out but herself. Betty is her friend of whom she would never say anything negative, except whenever Betty is not around. But that's okay. Betty is used to the negative energy. In fact she is a power generator for it. She would not tell anyone to get lost – instead with one look she'd make you feel like nail fungus. If you are brave enough to ask her about her love life, she will tell you straight up that there are no good men left.

No worries though. The evening is about to begin. The leader moves through a few praise choruses, and you mumble the words. Quietly, you admit to yourself that you would not be doing the church thing in the middle of the week if you were married. You turn to your left to see "Busy Bob" playing with his palm pilot in the middle of the song. Usually he does not come to these meetings because he is, well, busy, usually working twice the hours you work each week. Much of it is overtime. It's not because the company needs it, but "If you are not committed to your job, than get out of the way and let somebody else have it." He is here tonight because somebody more committed took his job, or because he has a birthday coming up and is getting anxious about his age.

He is sitting next to "Computer Carl." Carl is up on all the latest Bible software and is part of the audio ministry at church. He never has a bad thing to say about anybody, but that is because he does not interact much with people. Computers are far more interesting and much more manageable. He is the guy to call when your PC turns against you, but when you begin to share on a personal level, you get the feeling Carl's emotional mainframe shut down a long time ago. His answers are binary and his empathy is short-circuited. Two minutes into any conversation and he needs to be rebooted.

The speaker begins the lesson for the night: the topic is about living for God rather than living for yourself. Real Christianity means feeding the homeless, showing up for the deacon's work day, and constantly sharing Christ with people. This is what God wants out of you. Anything *you* might want is selfish, so give it up. Singles have more time than married people so they should be doing more. Throughout the message "Ministry Martha" is nodding her head with approval. When you ask her if she is dating anyone, she responds, "Right now I'm dating Jesus." As the speaker closes in prayer you think about what a lazy Christian you have been again this week. Maybe you will get it right next week.

You spend the rest of the evening standing around with a Styrofoam cup in your hand trying to look poised, content, and impressive. You watch "Desperate Deke" try to recapture his youth with "Devastated Danielle." Deke never tires of telling you how he is more godly than his ex-wife, and Danielle had her heart broken by Jack, so she is not ready for love right now. Of course she and Jack broke up nine years ago, but one cannot rush the healing process.

You try to strike up a conversation with "Wallflower Wilma," but she seems intimidated by the fact that you even acknowledged her. Her eyes target your shoes and she answers all your questions with "uh-huhs" or "if you say so's." "Wealthy William" interrupts your non-conversation to show you his new videophone with which he promises to send you

Chapter Two – Identity

pictures of his new and bigger house; but then he remembers and reminds you that you do not have a videophone to receive the pictures.

Reaching your breaking point you pitch the Styrofoam cup that you have been crushing with your hands and head to the exit. You skillfully avoid "My Past is too Painful Pauline" and "Recapture my Youth Roger" on the way out. Finally making it to your car you drive away shaking your head in frustration – frustration with the evening and with yourself for playing the part of "Resentful Reader." You will try something different next week, maybe "Bubbly Bibliophile" or "Bombastic Bookworm."

Okay, so I am exaggerating a little bit here. Yet, my point is that because we singles are missing that special person in our lives, and because God's timing is not what we always prefer, the temptation is strong to recast ourselves into a more functional identity – an identity we can control. Yet the mask we don always limits rather than liberates.

LET'S MAKE A DEAL

For years I lived as "Performance Pete." Somewhere in the deep recesses of my heart I conceived the idea that if I was really good and did all the things that a good Christian should do, then God would hold up His end of the deal. His end, of course, was to give me whatever I wanted, whenever I wanted it, and to spare me from any significant disappointments in life.

In effect I was saying, "God I will forego growth and maturity if you just give me two or three small things." I did not want to be a powerful CEO, a multimillionaire, or a professional football player. What I wanted was much more respectable and religious. I was willing to do plenty of Bible study, attend church regularly, be nice to old ladies, and floss daily if He would just give me an easy life, a house with a white picket fence, and a wife. "Performance Pete" would perform really well for God and in return all he wanted was for God to do the same.

However, this plan had one minor problem. God did not keep up His end of the bargain. He let the ball drop. But that is because He never agreed to my arrangement in the first place. He saw through my attempt to control my life and would never sign on to such a deal. Now I realize I had tried to trade sonship for slavery. Even though it appeared religious, I was avoiding a relationship with my God.

Gradually I have learned that God wants to give me so much more. He does not want me for what I can do for Him. He did not save me so that both of us can follow through on a contract conceived in distrust. He saved me and loves me because He wants me to be His child. A slave lives under fear and limitations. A servant lives under rules to receive a wage. A son lives in the freedom and love of a benevolent Father.

The number one problem with the human race is that we do not know who we are. In our confusion and deliberate rejection of the truth we attempt to create for ourselves a worthy identity. We reject the identity God has given us and repackage ourselves according to our liking. It may be an identity to win people or push them away, but it is a concerted effort to stabilize ourselves and control our surroundings. Any such identity is always conceived in sin.

Surely the angels were confused when Adam and Eve started to believe that they were lacking something. The proposition the Evil One made them in the garden was more than just about fruit: the serpent won them to his cause when he offered them a new identity.

> *God knows that your eyes will be opened when you eat it. You will become just like God, knowing everything, both good and evil.*
> - (Gen. 3:5b)

The first couple came to believe that who they were in truth was not as great as who they could be. The promise that eating the fruit would change their identity was true. The promise that it would be a better identity was a lie. With just one bite, Adam and Eve stepped down as the royalty of creation to become walking corpses. Every time we forget we are the image bearers of the Great King and pretend to be someone else, we make the same choice.

Singles have a unique window of time in their lives and should take advantage of this gift. They have presumably left the immaturity of adolescence behind and do not have to meet the demands of a spouse, children, or in-laws. Most likely they have the time, money, and freedom to do whatever they want. So why not ignore the approval ratings of others and live out our God-given design? Because, like everyone else, we have forgotten that who we really are makes the angels blush.

KINGDOM IDENTITIES

God did not create Adam and Eve simply because He needed some professional landscaping done. He formed these incarnations of His strength and beauty to represent His authority throughout the earth. God's throne is in heaven, but the goal from the beginning was to extend His heavenly rule and kingdom throughout the earth. His image bearers would be the breathing, walking, and talking reminders throughout the land that the Great King rules above. And as God ruled above, they would bear His image below.

Richard Pratt elaborates on what it means to be God's image bearers in his book, *Designed for Dignity*.

> *Moses and his Israelite readers understood these words because they lived in a world full of images. The most dominant images in the cultures of the ancient Near East were those of kings. Throughout the ancient world, kings made images of themselves and placed them in various locations in their kingdoms. Pharaohs of Egypt, the Emperors of Babylon, and the kings of other empires used images of themselves to display their authority and power.*
>
> *This custom of Moses' day helped him understand why God called Adam and Eve his image. Just as human kings had their images, the divine King ordained that the human race would be his royal image. Put simply, the expression 'image of God' designated human beings as representatives of the supreme King of the universe.*

Wow. Really? I bet you did not realize you were reading a book written by a representative of the supreme King of the universe. Perhaps you have forgotten that you are one too. That is a heck of a lot better than being "Marry-Me Molly" or "Computer Carl." It is also a whole lot better than letting your singleness define your identity.

Chapter Two – Identity

It is no small thing to be the representative of the king of the universe. Earthly rulers carefully pick who will represent them, and the Great King is no different. The creatures bearing His image must be the pinnacle of His creation. They must inspire respect in the rest of God's creatures. They must be grand figures who represent their Sovereign's wisdom, mystery, imagination, and pleasures. They are powerful yet tender, wise yet humble, simple yet dynamic, and confident yet worshipful. They are a little below the angels and the vice-regents of creation. They are princes or princesses in a loving relationship with their benevolent Father. This is who you were created to be, and it is the only identity you need.

The single's joy comes from knowing the benefits of belonging to the Great King. His children have received His smile so they know they are the offspring of royalty. They do not live like stable hands or milkmaids because that is not who they are. They are clothed in the colors of royalty, they explore the land with confidence, and they live for the praise of no man because they have the blessing of the King. They are free to approach Him whenever they wish with whatever concerns them at the moment. They are not afraid to enter battle because the armies of the King always go with them. They obey the King's commands because they believe the Sovereign of the realm knows best. They do not worry when they are falsely accused, ridiculed, mocked, or hurt by others because their Father will take up their cause. They are free to explore, experience, risk, fail, petition, rejoice, love, and live because they are the delight of the highest authority in the land. Only a prince or princess has such a marvelous identity!

What would it mean for our lives if we remembered our kingdom identity as a prince or princess? We would surrender our attempts to control everything and let our Father show us our place in the land. We would overcome our fear of others and certain situations because we would remember who we are. We would stop trying to figure everything out, stop demanding God do things our way, and stop insisting that He get with the program. The goal of our lives would no longer be marriage; we would drop the church-hopping looking for potentials and relinquish our demanding spirit regarding our future spouse.

Children of the Great King are not afraid to enlarge their desires; they want more out of life because they know their Father only gives them the very best. They are comfortable taking a risk because the King makes all things work together for good, and if they fail, it does not make them a failure. They are royalty. Remember? They can be bold for their Father and walk confidently among the servants because they are confident in who they are. And when they grow weary from fighting the King's enemies they do not need to wait for a royal summons to walk boldly into the throne room, past all the other servants, to receive their Father's full attention. He embraces His children as they weep and speaks to them of His love and the glory to come.

I have a vision of alive and passionate singles who live out the gospel in freedom and radical love - singles who exhibit a contagious strength and beauty that captivates the world. Singles who know the pain of loneliness and heartache, but each day choose again to live in hope. If that sounds out of this world, then it is. But, of course, so was Jesus' kingdom.

What would it look like for you to live out your kingdom identity? What if you courageously took the mask off and let us see the face that is really you? If you think you are too boring, too weak, too ugly, or too stupid to show, than you are still wearing the mask. The real you is a royal and majestic image of the Sovereign who makes creation gasp in awe.

So how about it guys? What would it look like for you to respond completely to the gospel and come fully alive? How would you live out the God-given strength in your heart? Jesus could really use some bad boys for His kingdom. Whose approval would you stop seeking? What fears would you look in the eye? How would you walk, talk, and dress? How would you love freely and radically? What would be uniquely attractive about you to both sexes? Do you really believe you are a prince and a son of the Great King?

Ladies? What would a heart fully alive look like for you? Do not follow someone else's footsteps; follow in the steps of Jesus that lead towards freedom, smiles, forgiveness, and intimacy. You have no idea what a powerful presence you have as the walking, breathing beauty images of God. How would truly believing that change your life? Not that I would know, but I would guess you'd want to toss your head at the Evil One and say with Shania Twain, "Man! I feel like a woman!" You are more than a woman. You are a princess, a daughter of the Great King.

So how about it? Break some of those arbitrary rules you have imposed on your life. Pursue Christ with reckless abandon. Tell an enemy you love them. Try something which you will possibly fail. Call a friend and ask for their forgiveness regardless of their response. Do something spontaneous without trying to control the situation. Buy a gift for someone without any valid reason. Ask God for something wild. Refuse to edit yourself for others. Cook something new. Encourage the person of whom you are jealous. Do something shocking. Turn up the music and dance. Love God and live as you please, for the good news is that your family is royalty and your home is a castle.

****

In the movie *Chocolat* a small French village is locked into a stale traditionalism that blunts the desires and hides the pain of its members. Authority is demanding, tradition is clear, clothing is bland, and routine is the norm. Neighbors live in suspicion and fear of one another. The local church supports this suffocating oppression, adding to it with outdated rituals, dry sermons, and endless, monotonous hymns. The entire village and its members' hearts could all be painted with dull browns and grays.

All of this changes when a mysterious woman and her daughter arrive in town one day. The woman opens a *chocolaterie* and begins serving the sensual delicacy to the town's inhabitants. But this is no ordinary chocolate - this is a special recipe that enlivens the passions of its partakers in unexpected and exciting ways. Eventually the entire town is transformed. People confront their private pain. Women stand up to their abusers. Relationships are restored. Even the village mayor, the strongest bulwark of tradition and control, comes to life. The closing scene of the film is an exuberant party in the village courtyard. Bright colors abound, smiles are everywhere, and people begin to really live for the first time.

Every time I watch this film I see a great analogy of the gospel. Before Christ came into our lives our souls were brown, gray, and dreary inside. There was nowhere to go with our pain, there was everything to fear, and passions were considered dangerous.

When Jesus comes into our hearts, He throws open the windows, dusts off the furniture, and redecorates with the vibrant and brilliant colors of passion, risk, friendship, laughter, and love. He is not the living chocolate, but He is the living water. Once you get a taste, you keep coming back for more.

The Single Journey

CHAPTER THREE

DREAMS

Dream on, dream on, dream on. Dream until your dreams come true
 - Aerosmith

The books or the music in which we thought the beauty was located will betray us if we trust to them; it was not in *them, it only came* through *them, and what came through them was longing. These things – the beauty, the memory of our own past – are good images of what we really desire; but if they are mistaken for the thing itself, they turn into dumb idols, breaking the hearts of their worshippers. For they are not the thing itself, they are only the scent of a flower we have not found, the echo of a tune we have not heard, news from a country we have never yet visited.*
 - C.S. Lewis, *The Weight of Glory*

Hope deferred makes the heart sick, but when dreams come true, there is life and joy.
 - (Proverbs 13:12)

In 1940 Walt Disney released his film version of the movie Pinocchio. It was not the first time the story of the wooden puppet was told, but it was, without question, its best telling. The advanced animation, expressive voices, and catchy songs made Disney's Pinocchio the only version of the story that people remember. Who can forget the tale of the loving puppet-master, Geppetto, who wants nothing more than his wooden puppet, Pinocchio, to become a real boy? One night a mysterious fairy queen answers his prayers and brings the wooden puppet to life, giving him a chance to prove his true character and become a real boy. Yet, despite his best efforts, his sidekick, Jiminy Cricket, cannot keep him out of trouble. Pinocchio falls into all kinds of dangers and corruption on Pleasure Island and finds the wild life is actually turning him into a jackass, literally. Only after saving his father, Geppetto, from the mighty whale, Monstro, does the fairy queen allow Pinocchio to become a real boy. As the film credits role you can still hear the Academy Award-winning song in the background.

When you wish upon a star,
makes no difference who you are
Anything your heart desires
will come to you.

If your heart is in your dreams,
no request is too extreme
When you wish upon a star
as dreamers do.

Walt Disney earned a fortune by making films, recording songs, and constructing theme parks about our deepest dreams. The world of Disney invites us into an exciting world unlike our own. It is a world of dramatic places, brave heroes, innocent damsels, dastardly villains, and dangerous

Chapter Three – Dreams

swordfights. Beasts turn into bachelors as they learn to love, sleeping beauties awake with but a kiss, spotted dogs experience an exciting adventure to escape an erratic woman, sorcerers are destroyed with a sword, foxes become friends with hounds, and wooden puppets turn into real boys. You may think yourself too old for cartoons, but something in these stories captivate us.

AWAKENED

I am often deeply moved each time I go to the movies. If I am not busy critiquing cinematography or the screenwriting, then I tend to get caught up in the story. It is rare that I leave a film and do not find myself awakened by an actor's line or by a particular scene. A dangerous mission or ambitious quest always stirs my interest. A strong hero who faces a daunting challenge and learns much about himself along the way is a story I want to be my own. A bad guy who plots evil at the expense of the hero's peace is a plot line that resonates as true. Throw in a pounding soundtrack, a breathtaking setting, and a beautiful woman and I am hooked. No wonder John Eldredge calls movies a "window to the heart."

I experience a similar longing when I watch music videos. I believe that God has given us music as a foretaste of heaven. Great music is even more powerful when it is mixed with entrancing images. I particularly enjoy videos that tell a short story. *How will he get her back? How did she get to this place in life? Where did they first fall in love? What is he willing to do for her?* Everyone seems so talented and good-looking in the videos. They sing on bridges, in canyons, and at hopping clubs. Nothing about their lives is boring. They are passionately in love with passionate mates. Something inside me says this is how life is supposed to be – exciting, passionate, romantic. Where can I get this life? Is it only in music videos?

When I went to the mall today, I found myself asking the same questions. In search of a pair of sunglasses, as soon as I opened the door I felt like I was floating through another reality. All my senses were tantalized from every direction. The latest fragrances threatened to sedate me. I could hear the sounds of the exciting new release in the video store and the inviting beat of the latest hit album in the music store. I could not walk past the food court without inhaling aromas that tickled my taste buds. The wakeboards and surfboards in the beach shop reminded me of the thrill of water sports. Everywhere I looked, I saw people wearing great clothes, smiling and laughing, and being with people who looked like a lot of fun. The guys were buffed, strong, and confident and the women, at least in one store window, were... well... umm... perfect. Enchanted by this world portrayed before me, I left with the lingering thought, "*Why can't my life be more like that?*"

Can our lives be more like the reality that is played out before us at the mall, in music videos, and at the movies? Do our lives have to be such a boring contrast to that kind of excitement? Are we really missing a life full of action, excitement, and romance? In short, can we live the life of our wildest dreams? I believe the answer is yes and no.

The answer is no because when I walk through the mall and my senses and emotions are swept away, I am succumbing to crass commercialism and marketing. The same items that are screaming, "See how great I am!" are also screaming, "Buy me! Buy several of me!" - that is never good for my self-esteem or my wallet. Our culture also sells the lie that more is better; a full garage is the best garage and a wardrobe purchased yesterday is already too old. The world of movies and music videos is a sham in many respects. It is amazing what lighting, makeup, 33 retakes, studio editing, and well-rehearsed lines can do to make anybody look good. The truth is our lives will not be glutted with happiness until heaven comes to earth, and so I will speak about heaven in a moment. In the meantime the entire creation groans for the return of Christ.

Yet there is something real to the desires that the mall and media awaken within me. Behind all the materialism and glamour, I thirst for a deeper and richer life, a life that is not filled with watching reruns on TV, taking naps, or complaining about people. It is a life of drama, beauty, imagination, victory, and romance. It is a life in which I am caught up into something important, my role matters in the great story - and my life is worth living. To find such a life is like finding a treasure buried in a field. Without hesitation, I am willing to sell all that I have to possess this treasure. It is a life found only in my wildest dreams.

AND THEN?

My friend Larry is a highly successful counselor who sees a long list of clients each week. He told me recently that many of his clients come to him not because of serious problems requiring medical attention, but because they are struggling with mild depression and pervasive boredom. Often the first question Larry asks them is what they dreamed about and loved to do when they were young. Usually the answers include fishing, singing, playing baseball, writing, sailing, or dancing. Yet, when Larry asks his clients to recall the last time they did the things they loved, they struggle to remember. He lets his clients figure out for themselves that they are not doing what they love. In short, they are not pursuing their dreams.

It is strange that singles who usually have more time and money than others need to be reminded of the same thing. Why would the most creative, mobile, and capable group in the church need to be told that they do not want enough out of life? Because most singles have developed a one-track mind with only one dream that becomes a goal, that one goal becomes an obsession, and that obsession becomes an addiction that weighs them down.

The lone dream is, of course, a spouse. Now there is nothing wrong with this dream. For most of us, to stifle the dream for an intimate marriage is to lie to our own hearts. The dream for lasting love is one of God's greatest gifts, but the crippling inclination of many singles is to toss out all other desires in pursuit of this one goal.

I fear that many singles have come to believe the lie that the goal of their life is to get "unsingled." I say unsingled rather than married because such folks are often trying to move *away* from something rather than genuinely move *towards* someone. They are seeking relief from loneliness, boredom, and depression rather than pursuing intimate, committed, and sacrificial relationships which characterize a healthy marriage. Those who seek to be unsingled are like the Cookie Monster – obsessed with only one thing.

In the film *Mona Lisa Smile*, Julia Roberts plays a progressive art history teacher named Katherine Watson, who takes a teaching position at the 1950's conservative Wellesley College in Massachusetts. She quickly attracts the attention of her students and the college administration because of her affection for modern art and contemporary thinking. She is a

Chapter Three – Dreams

1960's feminist teaching in a college with 1950's values. She despairs over the limited vision of her female students who are more concerned with finding husbands than in sharpening their minds and pursuing their full potential. At one point in the film, Ms. Watson reads the student file of Joan, played by Julia Stiles.

MS. WATSON:	It says here that you are pre-law. What law school are you going to go to?
JOAN:	I hadn't really thought about that. I mean after I graduate I plan on getting married.
MS. WATSON:	And then?
JOAN:	(Confused) …Aannnnd thennn… I'll be married.
MS. WATSON:	You can do both… Just for fun if you could go to any school in the country which would it be?
JOAN:	(Excited) Yale… Yale. They keep five slots open for women. One unofficially for a Wellesley girl.
MS. WATSON:	But you hadn't really thought about it.

Sadly many singles think only about getting married. Even though God has placed a multitude of desires on their hearts, they allow only one desire to consume them. They stay inside and watch the clock on the wall when they could go outside and play. All my married friends remind me that people who are lonely, bored, and directionless when they are single are even more lonely, bored, and directionless when they are married. Getting unsingled does not solve their problems. It only makes them worse.

When I let feelings of loneliness pull me down into despair and hopelessness, I become a rather unattractive and boring person. My friends roll their eyes and look at their watches hoping to escape another depressing conversation with me. During several of these pity parties God has confronted me with Ms. Watson's same question: *And then? If I miraculously gave you a mate today, Pete, then what would you do with your life? Would you enter a nursing home and wait to die because the goal of your life was accomplished?* Okay, so He did not say it quite like that, but I fear sometimes that I would be willing to make that trade.

Put the book down for a moment and ask yourself the same question, "And then?" If you got married today and started a new life with a spouse what would you do then? If you just plan on living off the love then you need more help than this book can give you. I am sure if you tried, you could name quite a few married people who are bored with life and each other. Will you join them one day? If you have stopped dreaming dreams other than marriage then you are already there. When we turn our singleness into our primary identity, we lose our ability to listen to the many dreams and desires that God has written on our hearts. When we focus on only one of our desires, and allow it to consume us, we miss out on the abundant life found in Christ.

This may come as a radical surprise, but God cares deeply about each of our dreams and desires. *"He delights in every detail of their lives."* (Ps. 37:23) He knows how much a spouse would mean to us, but He is faithful and gracious to remind us of our other dreams, even when we are intent on leaving them in the dust. We may only want a wedding, but God wants us to have a wedding and a whole lot more. Once again single Christians do not want enough out of life.

DREAMY SINGLES

I was recently invited by friends at church to join a men's group that met each Tuesday night. I knew some of the guys before I joined, but most were strangers. On the first night we were encouraged to formulate a list of our goals and dreams to share with the others. It was an opportunity to listen to our hearts, to take stock of where we were going in life, and to get to know each other a little better. I listened as each guy shared his desire for travel, ministry, and friendship. Dale wanted to take his mom to England. Jim's eyes got wider when he talked about climbing the Tetons. Mitch expressed a desire to mentor younger guys into manhood. As the rest shared their dreams we would often pause to affirm, question, or encourage one another.

As the latecomer, I would be the last guy to share in the group. I looked forward to sharing with great anticipation, and as my night approached, I kept reminding myself to sit down and write out my dreams. Most of the guys had shared 15-20 dreams so I knew I needed to set aside enough time to get in that range as well. Days passed and still I had not taken the time to sit and write.

Finally, I put a pen to paper. As a night owl, I prefer to wake up at about 9:30 a.m. each morning, but for some reason God woke me up at 5:00 a.m. and freed me to dream. (I believe

The Single Journey

God speaks to His children at night and in the morning, but if I am really honest He speaks a little louder if you get up early to hear Him). After an hour and a half, I had listed 77 dreams! That is some pretty fast dreaming, but I knew when I was done that I had poured out my heart on those pages, just as Hannah had poured out her heart before the Lord (I Sam. 1:15).

I want to share some of the dreams on my list in hopes of inspiring you. I tried to include character, physical, mental, social, and spiritual goals, but more than anything I placed no restrictions on my heart and just wrote freely, without the slightest hesitation. I am too embarrassed to share goals #12, #50, and #77, but here are several from the list:

#2.	Scuba dive The Great Barrier Reef
#14.	Eat a meal at every Hard Rock Café in the world (11 so far!)
#19.	Take a road trip of the UK and stay at local bed and breakfasts
#21.	Write a biography on Oliver Cromwell
#44.	Lose my propensity to worry
#48.	Learn how to flip my wakeboard
#52.	Witness the Red Sox beat the Yankees and go on to win the World Series*
#59.	Love and give proactively before the other person
#68.	Teach a class on the history of rock n' roll
#75.	Visit my friend, Collin, who is a missionary in Africa

* *This dream was fulfilled in October 2004!*

Now of course I did not forget my desire to be married. Dream #7 is "marry the right woman at the right time." But I am trying to see this dream as one of many dreams for my life. Marriage is very important to me, but it is not the sole focus of my life. I encourage you to get away to one of your favorite secluded spots and make your own list of dreams. Ask God to bring the desires of your heart to the surface. Listen to what He has placed within you and write it down. Be bold and courageous and even embarrass yourself, but do not think for a second that any of your dreams are silly to God. Often the most quirky aspects of our heart best reflect who we really are.

One note about pursuing your dreams. I often hear singles complain that they would do more if they had more money. Singles are funny with money. They simultaneously overspend and under-spend. Often they have the money to do what they want, but they are spending it in other places. Take another look at your budget and see if you are wasting quarters while claiming you only have nickels to follow your dreams.

DEFERRED DREAMS

For a brief period of time in college I had plans of being an English major. I figured getting paid to read and teach cool stories would be a great way to make a living. I signed up for as many courses as my schedule would allow. I filled my head with Chaucer, Hawthorne, Shakespeare, and Conrad. I was hooked and headed towards a life of character analysis and authorial interpretation, until I took an introductory course in poetry. I have always appreciated rhyme, meter, alliteration, and onomatopoeia, but the poems we read were so bizarre! Poems about wet wheelbarrows, bullets penetrating skulls, and absurd fantasies of drug addicts were not what I had in mind. To further sour the experience, my professor was an older woman with gray frizzy hair who believed it was still 1968. She kept saying, "Isn't this brilliant? Isn't this brilliant?" Maybe with some LSD I would have appreciated the classics a little more, but I was a poor college student who could not afford the street price of LSD. Instead, I changed my major.

The poetry class was not a total loss, however. I discovered a poem I have loved since the first time I read it. The poem was written by Langston Hughes, an African-American writer in 1920's Harlem, entitled "A Dream Deferred."

> *What happens to a dream deferred?*
> *Does it dry up*
> *like a raisin in the sun?*
> *Or fester like a sore-*
> *And then run?*
> *Does it stink like rotten meat?*
> *Or crust and sugar over-*
> *like a syrupy sweet?*
> *Maybe it just sags*
> *like a heavy load.*
> *Or does it explode?*

I am not quite sure if Langston Hughes was talking about one specific dream when he wrote this poem. Perhaps he was struggling to understand the American Dream, or maybe the dream of civil rights for all African-Americans. I like to think that he was referring to dreams in general, and asked some powerful questions about dreams gone unfulfilled.

If something is deferred, it is "put off" or "delayed" or even "yielded." What happens to unfulfilled dreams? What happens when something or someone we earnestly long for is denied to us? To rejoice when our expectations are met is easy.

Chapter Three – Dreams

We ask few philosophical questions at that point. But what about when things do not go the way we want? When years pass and frustration grows, what then? I think this poem offers insight.

Some dreams change. They are like grapes that dry up in the sun and become raisins. I love grapes. They are colorful, sweet, and juicy. They are delicious, but so are raisins. Raisins have a stranger taste than grapes and certainly look different, but I enjoy a handful of raisins as much as I do a handful of grapes. The two are not the same, but one becomes the other.

The same is true of some of our dreams. Sometimes one dream changes into another. When my friend Luke was in high school he wanted to be a cop like his dad and brothers. That dream did not work out, but today he is the principal of a local middle school and loves his job. The dream changed shape, but still brought satisfaction.

When we are young we dream boldly. Boys want to be astronauts, soldiers, and race car drivers. Girls want to be dancers, singers, or runway models. Are the boys that grow up to be astronauts the only ones faithful to their dreams? Are the little girls who become Miss America more faithful to their dreams than other girls? I do not think so. Much of what we desire and dream about when we are young is a temporary reflection of who we really are. How the dream gets fulfilled may look different than how it was originally conceived, but what is important is the *desire* behind many of our dreams. When my friend Larry was young he wanted to be a quarterback so he could lead a team of men. Today he is not a quarterback of a professional football team, but he is a counselor who leads men on wilderness retreats to hunt and fish. When I was young I pretended I was Superman and Spider-man because I wanted to be a hero and fight for what was right. I did not grow up to wear tights, but God has blessed me with an opportunity to fight for the hearts and souls of His people through writing and teaching. It is okay that some of our dreams change. We did not sell out along the way; rather it is God's way of giving us what we need instead of what we think we want.

Some dreams fester like a sore and then run. That sounds pretty disgusting, but it is true. A sore is an abnormal growth on the body that swells and soon demands our attention. If untreated, it will putrefy and run with pus. When we recast our dreams or desires as our identities, then they become like sores on the body. To become obsessed with a dream is to turn it into an addiction.

My first scuba instructor had always dreamed of opening his own dive shop. He was very experienced and highly knowledgeable, and nobody would have doubted his skill as a diver. Yet, it was evident that his identity was tied into his ability as a diver. He could be very patronizing when answering questions. He frequently mentioned all the places he had dived, what he had accomplished, and how he was a better instructor than others. When he did make a mistake he became defensive and irritable. I wonder if he ever considered dreaming new dreams, or was he determined to be known only for what he could do best? When we are addicted to only one job, hobby, or person, we stifle our ability to grow and experience new things. Our dreams become festering sores.

Some dreams smell like rotten meat. This is another distasteful image, but I think the poem is saying that some dreams are good for awhile, but then they rot and need to be thrown away. In other words some dreams die. Sometimes we are responsible for the deaths of our own dreams. We are faithless and doubt that God is good, so we refuse to give Him our hearts. We secretly long for wonderful things, but do not think God cares and so we give up. We kill our aspirations to advance and move the kingdom of God. We surrender our desires to experience bold new adventures and we pretend not to want deep and intimate relationships. Our dreams die because it is too hard to keep believing. Yet, each time a dream dies, so does a piece of our hearts.

I have found that part of God's sanctifying work in my life is to revive the dreams I have allowed to die. All the time God is calling to mind dreams or desires that I have given up out of frustration or fear. I have always dreamed of being a writer, yet I fought God when He began moving me towards this career. When I am quiet before Him, He often asks, "What about this desire or that dream? Do you trust me enough to bring before me all your dreams?" I have to confess that often my answer is no. My faithlessness turns my dreams into rotting meat.

However there is another reason why so many dreams die. Despite a devout response to the gospel and our desire to live passionate and abundant lives, we still live in a fallen world with corruptible bodies. If we are honest we must admit that we live in a very sad world. Listen to all the pain around you. Think of the loved ones lost to sickness and death at an early age. Consider the marriages full of resentment and unhappiness. How many people do you know who are addicted to alcohol, consumed with pornography, weakened by an eating disorder, wounded from sexual abuse, defeated by depression, or paralyzed by their pasts? I know too many. Sometimes I cannot help but grieve over all this destruction. I would be a fool to glibly suggest that all this pain could be overcome if people just held onto their dreams. There may be some truth there, but the harsh reality is that we are not yet home. Heaven – not earth - is where *all* our dreams come true. For now the sin and horror of this world will often get in the way of our greatest dreams and crush our spirits. Our dreams sometimes rot because we are living on a rotting planet. We eagerly await the day when Jesus will return and give us the lives of our wildest dreams.

Do some dreams "crust and sugar over like a syrupy sweet?" I think so. Some dreams go unfulfilled, but it is okay. The relationship you thought was going to be "the one" falls apart, but you know it is for the best. You get passed over for the promotion you thought you deserved, but it is alright because it would have meant more stress. Last year I applied for a job in Nashville, Tennessee. I was excited about the job and the prospect of living in the music city, but my phone never rang. They did not even care to interview me. But it was okay because it would have meant a big move, and God was blessing me in new ways in Florida. This is different from giving up a dream when things get tough. I am talking about a quiet and restful assurance that if things do not go as we hoped, we can remember our Father is still busy working what is good in our lives, turning something crusty into something syrupy sweet.

Of course there are dreams that sag like a heavy load – the kind that remain unfulfilled year after year. I admit these are the toughest ones for me. If you are reading this book, then marriage is probably the dream that lingers year after year on your heart and goes unfulfilled. The assaults of the Evil One can be overwhelming. Sometimes he whispers, *"Why do you think God would bless you with a spouse after all these years? He decided to keep you single a long time ago, can't you take a hint? Who would want to marry you anyway? Do you really think you will ever find someone to fall in love with?"* I find that God uses these dreams, and particularly my singleness, to accomplish His most extensive work in me. It is not easy, but when dreams linger year after year, feeling like a sagging, heavy load, we must continue to bring them before our Father. He offers to replace our burden, which is heavy, with His burden, which is light.

Finally, and this is my favorite kind, there are dreams that explode. Only God can explode a dream. I do not mean that He obliterates our desires with TNT; nor does He destroy our spirits. When God explodes a dream He transforms a desire from the singular to the plural. He takes a solitary and specific desire, and makes it far grander in design, impact, and pleasure than we could have ever conceived. He is not satisfied with us saying, "I want this dream," and then giving us what we ask. Rather He says, "Not only will I give you that dream, but I will give you far more than you asked or anticipated." He gives us new experiences, new relationships, deeper growth, profound wisdom, another testimony of His love, and a life that deeply impacts people. A dream that God explodes far exceeds a solitary desire. It becomes a grand chapter in the story He is writing for our lives.

I moved to Florida to follow my dream of teaching. That dream was fulfilled with my job, but God also transformed my relationships and my heart in ways beyond what I had imagined. God has done far more than what I asked before I moved. Truly His ways are higher than our ways and His thoughts higher than our thoughts (Isa. 55:9).

FREE TO DREAM

So do Christians have a leg up over the world in pursuing their dreams? If all it takes to live an exciting life is to know our dreams and then follow them, then why do we need God? Because only those who are loved by an infinite love are truly free to dream. Only when we live in the love of the God of the universe, will we be comfortable living boldly. When we know that we are in good with the Great King we do not need to keep looking over our shoulders to see if we are going to get zapped. Succeed or fail, we know we are still the King's heirs. Without such liberating love our dreams become addictions, and addictions always chain our hearts. I kill my dreams when I think I am God's hired hand. I dream even bigger when I remember I walk free in His love as His adopted child.

What a great opportunity we have as singles to follow our dreams. So many of the grand projects and quirky desires that are written on our hearts can be explored and pursued. Marriage, as grand as it can be, will often put a pinch on many of our dreams. The responsibilities and sacrifices we will have to meet in marriage are obviously not here now. How sad if we wait for life to happen to us instead of us happening to life.

There is no question that my dream for an intimate marriage is at the top of my list; but as long as I am still single I intend to pursue my wildest dreams. And when I do get married I hope to meet the responsibilities of that relationship while at the same time awakening new desires and dreaming new dreams. Pursuing our dreams is not just something we do until marriage. It is what we do with God's grace as long as we have breath. So follow Aerosmith's advice: Dream on and on and on, and when you do get married, then dream some more.

CHAPTER FOUR

FRIENDS

There are no ordinary people. You have never talked to a mere mortal.
— C.S. Lewis, *The Weight of Glory*

Your friend is the man who knows all about you, and still likes you.
— Elbert Hubbard

I will thank the Lord with all my heart as I meet with his godly people.
— (Ps. 111:1)

    In the spring of 2004 one of the most successful series in television history came to an end. For ten years the cast of *Friends* captured the essence of what it meant to be single in the big city. The show addressed many of the unique issues singles face and did so with humor and style. It took me longer than most singles to become a fan of the show. In fact, I did not even care to watch it until I gained a deeper appreciation of its characters. Eventually I could see why millions of other fans cheered for the cast. They were characters with whom we could easily identify.

The Single Journey

We all knew someone like Joey, the baby-faced Italian, who did not enjoy the same success with his work as he did with his women. Ross, the odd paleontologist, had a good heart, but was oh so frustrated in his desire to be married. Chandler's humor lightened the tension in any scene, but we knew his humor covered a lot of his own private confusion. Every control freak met their match in Monica, and every fashion queen found their heroine in Rachel. And just in case you forgot it was a sitcom, Phoebe would leave you shaking your head. However out of touch you were, she was still one step behind. Any combination of these friends at Central Perk Coffee Shop was the perfect recipe for plenty of laughs and memorable conversations.

Perhaps the show made the single life out to be more glamorous than it usually feels, but it did capture what it meant to be single at the turn of the century. The struggle for a career, the disappointments of dating, the stress of roommates, and the need for close relationships struck a cord with the growing single population. More than anything the show revealed that even if your career was floundering, your parents were clueless, your past was a mess, and true love was nowhere in sight, everything would be more or less okay at the end of the day if you had great friends.

The search for friends like those on *Friends* is endless. The characters in the series were beautiful, dynamic, funny, loyal, and uninhibited. Who would not want to be part of their circle? When I look at my friends, I wonder why they cannot be more like those on TV. Often they do not meet my expectations and make me question why I even hang out with them. Of course the irony is that they would say the same thing about me. *Why can't Pete be more accepting, understanding, and flexible? Why does he persist with the same annoying patterns?* And so the search continues for each single to find those who consistently understand, affirm, and support them, people worthy to be their friends, people who, when they are honest for a moment, are just like them.

I'LL BE THERE FOR YOU ... MAYBE

Two of the most common sentiments in singles groups are resentment and toleration. An underlying bitterness exists in many church groups because, truth be told, hardly anyone *really* wants to be there. Singleness has become an unexpected detour in life and it is easy to take it out on others – often those closest to us. If you are like me, then you have always thought you were in control of your life. Only losers do not get married. How is it that you have been lumped together with people who have been run over by life and probably will remain single forever?

Most singles are simply waiting to find their mate so that when they do they can skip town, or at least their peer group, and never have to deal with those people again. Then they can be the one giving patronizing speeches about waiting for the right one because they now have it "figured out." As a consequence, I have talked to several female singles who have felt rejected by other singles in their church. Perhaps women see each other as competition. The guys on the other hand either retreat from girls, or hunt them like birds of prey. Guys in a group of singles are often reluctant to pursue a connection with other guys because what they really want is a girl. The fact that they are gradually becoming another friendless American male does not seem to bother them.

The inability of singles to connect is often revealed in something as simple as making plans for the weekend. If there is one idolatrous temple that singles visit more than any other, it is the one dedicated to the god of schedule. We can become so attached to our freedom, to come and go as we please, that we sacrifice spontaneity, new experiences, and meeting new people. I have often called friends to simply go to a movie on a Saturday night and I have been barraged with a sea of questions. *Who is going? Will Kurt be there? I am not going unless Katie goes. Do we all have to see the same movie? What if I meet up with you after dinner? Can you go to the theater closer to my house?* After a round of multiple phone calls, I have often thrown up my hands in disgust at singles' attempt to control every situation.

Jealousy can also be a painful issue among singles. We promise to be there for each other, through thick and thin, but when someone has a date on Valentine's Day, and we don't, suddenly our relationships turn sour.

I wish I could say I was innocent in all these categories, but I am not. My friend, Luke, and I were roommates for three years. During those years we grew close to each other and had a lot of great laughs. We traveled across country twice and served together in ministry. We frequently prayed, offering each other's requests before God, together and privately. I know of few roommates who have had a relationship as compatible as Luke and I.

It just so happened that when I bought a house and moved out Luke started dating the girl that would eventually become his wife. At long last my prayers for him were being answered. Luke was a new man. He could not stop smiling. The

Chapter Four – Friends

two of them were inseparable, destined for the altar from the beginning.

So how did I handle it? Did I come alongside my long-time friend to encourage and support him? Was I quick to rejoice with my friend in his rejoicing? Hardly - I developed reasons to isolate myself. I was busy with my house. I was busy with my work. I had a lot going on at church. My schedule was too full to get together, even though I lived only four streets away. I am ashamed to say that it took far too long for me to confess my bitterness towards him and God, all because Luke was experiencing something that I wanted to experience as well. Though my repentance was a long time in coming, when God finally broke me of my resentment I was free to love my friend again. I invited Luke and his fiancée over for dinner one night and we had a great evening. I am now honestly looking forward to the day of their wedding.

NORMAL PEOPLE

David and Jonathan had one of the deepest friendships in biblical history. Their story has always captured me. These two warriors were so intent on spending time together that they would sneak behind the king's back at the risk of their own lives. Their commitment to one another ran so deep that it seems almost trite to simply call them friends. In fact, they took a vow before the Lord to watch over each other's descendants, should one of them die. The Bible says that they loved each other more than they loved themselves. Upon their final meeting, knowing for the sake of the kingdom that they would have to part ways, they both broke down and wept. Shortly after their separation, Jonathan was killed in battle and David was consumed with grief over the loss of his beloved friend.

The Single Journey

How I weep for you, my brother Jonathan! Oh, how much I loved you! And your love for me was deep, deeper than the love of women!

- (II Samuel 1:26)

For many years I have read the story of David and Jonathan's friendship and longed for similar relationships in my own life. Recently, I re-read the story and noticed something new: if there were ever two individuals in ancient Israel with a legitimate excuse to hate each other, it would be these two. Jonathan was the son of King Saul and, therefore, the heir to the throne. Once his father died he would inherit the kingdom along with its wealth, power, and fame. The only people Jonathan had to look out for were those who would try to usurp his right to the throne.

David was such an individual. In fact, it was common knowledge in Israel that God had rejected Saul as king, and the prophet had anointed David as heir to the throne. The dynasty of Saul would begin and end with Saul. Jonathan's father was an embarrassment to Jonathan wherever he went. Surely people goaded Jonathan with the fact that he would never inherit the throne. He knew that God had passed over his family in favor of a scruffy, unknown, shepherd boy. If Jonathan held an intense hatred for David, and even sought to end his life, we would certainly understand.

Instead, Jonathan's friendship with David is unforgettable. Jonathan knew it was God's will for David to be king and did everything he could to protect him. I cannot get some singles to sit in a movie theater together, yet these guys promised to love each other even beyond death.

I think God snuck up behind me with this great story to show me something about my own life. When people fail to meet my needs, I have a tendency to label them as "not my type." I find reasons to avoid engaging with certain people because they fail to affirm me like I expect, or they do not do things the way I want them done. If there were ever two individuals that had an excuse to avoid friendship it was David and Jonathan. Yet, I often hold back from making such a deep commitment - do not expect too much from me when you are in need, I just might not be there for you.

Perhaps singles tend to ostracize because we believe there are normal people and abnormal people. The people just like us are the normal people, and everybody else is abnormal. If we can just find plenty of normal people then everything will be great and we will not have to deal with anyone else. Of course we will not run the abnormal people over with our cars, or spit on them in public, but neither do we have to bother inviting them for dinner or seek to meet their needs. They are just not like us so we can ignore them.

This kind of thinking is a far cry from the approach to relationships modeled by Jesus. And it is exactly what the Apostle Paul railed against in many of his letters. In fact, this type of factionalism in the church at Corinth provoked Paul to develop his famous analogy regarding the body of Christ (I Cor. 12:12-26). The church is like the human body made up of many parts. All the parts are important and each one is dependent upon the other. The hand cannot tell the eye to get lost, and the foot cannot tell the ear not to come for dinner. All the parts are important.

There is a reason for such diversity in God's church. We can all enrich one another. I am a better person because of the different types of people God has placed in my life. I am better off because of my relationship with Shawn, who models so much integrity and loyalty. I have learned how to confront awkward situations and difficult people through my friendship with Luke. My friend, Collin, is a wonderful example of what it means to seek first the kingdom of God. Neal consistently reminds me that everyday we are in a battle for our hearts.

I hate to think how immature I would be if these men of God were not also my friends. Life would have taken me down long ago without them. Yet all of these men are very different from me; none of them fit the mold of a "normal" person. Instead we are all slightly abnormal. The same is true of my other peers. I am slowly learning the wisdom of being around men and women with whom I have little in common, or who are nothing like me. If you find your list of friends to be rather short, ask yourself if you are only getting close to people who are "normal" – people just like yourself. If so, you may become quite bored. There is no golden friend out there who will never misunderstand, annoy, or disappoint you. The same is true of your future mate, so get used to it now.

There are no *normal* people. It is easy to label people in life as either important or unimportant. Certainly in the sea of faces you interact with each day, some are primary characters in your story and others are secondary, but none of them are irrelevant in God's eyes. C.S. Lewis said we have never spoken to a mere mortal; rather, if we truly considered the eternal destiny of the people we bump into each day then our dealings with them would be very different.

> *It may be possible for each to think too much of his own potential glory hereafter; it is hardly possible for him to think too often or too deeply about that of his neighbour. The load, or weight, or burden of my neighbour's glory should be laid on my back, a load*

Chapter Four – Friends

so heavy that only humility can carry it, and the backs of the proud will be broken. It is a serious thing to live in a society of possible gods and goddesses, to remember that the dullest and most uninteresting person you can talk to may one day be a creature which, if you saw it now, you would be strongly tempted to worship, or else a horror and a corruption such as you now meet, if at all, only in a nightmare. All day long we are, in some degree, helping each other to one or other of these destinations.

- (from *The Weight of Glory*)

If I could live with this perspective then I would think twice before dismissing someone because I am "too busy" and then run over to talk to somebody else. When I forget that other believers have a kingdom identity as well, I also forget the value they hold in the eyes of God. Even more, I may miss out on a great friendship. When I do not care that those outside of Christ will be cast from God's kingdom to destruction, then I am demonstrating a profound lack of love.

If you think your friends are too boring, too critical, too narrow, too afraid, or too anything then consider what they could be like with more of your encouragement and love. How would it impact your friends if they knew you would love them unconditionally, whether they fully understand and appreciate you or not? What are your friends afraid to speak to you about out of fear that you will reject their words? What are your friends afraid to be and do from lack of your support? We should never underestimate the effect our unconditional love could have on another life.

It is important to understand that though there are no normal or ordinary people, there are healthy and unhealthy people. A friendship with someone who pulls you towards defeat, lies, or sin is not a friendship – it is abuse. Unhealthy people demonstrate a consistent pattern of destruction and selfishness towards other people. Sometimes, separating yourself from such a person until they exhibit genuine change is the best way to be a friend to them.

CHOOSING TO CONNECT

You cannot make it on the single journey without a strong community of friends. The road is too long and hard to travel alone, and the loneliness will consume you along the way if you do not build solid relationships. The blessing of singleness is that we get to pick our community of friends by ourselves, and have the opportunity to learn about ourselves apart from a mate. This is a gift that married couples envy more than you realize. Moreover, the ability to be a strong friend is one of the strongest indicators of one's ability to develop a strong and healthy marriage. I want to share with you some of the best wisdom I have received on developing rich friendships.

We can easily buy into the lie that other people are content with their relationships and have no need for us. In reality, healthy people will never refuse one more friend. They are always looking for more people to connect with, more people to understand them, and more people to believe the best about them. Is that true of you? The best way to make friends is to be a great friend. You become irresistibly attractive to others when you strive to draw out the best in others. Let others know that you are cheering them on. When you see that they believe a lie about themselves, speak truth into their life. Strive to

Chapter Four – Friends

understand and appreciate their complexity. Let them know you believe in them and want the best for them.

In a cold world people will gather around warmth. We are naturally drawn to those people who are friendly. We cannot afford to be exclusive. If we are, then even the people in our circle will always be afraid of being cut from our roster. I once worked closely with a staff of eight people. When one person left the room the rest would speak poorly about that person. When he would return, another would leave and that person would become the target of attack. Everybody was nice to me when I was around, but I knew that I, too, was being slandered behind my back. I could not trust anyone in the office and had little respect for them. Build a reputation for extending the kindness of Christ to everyone. This will again mean associating with people who are not like you. But this is not some unique sacrifice you have to make in your single years. Unless you want an isolated and boring marriage you will need to appreciate abnormal people then as well. It is part of life and part of being a member of the body of Christ.

If you make it your objective to be a friend to everyone, then one of the highest hurdles you will need to overcome is the temptation to gossip. Unfortunately, the body of Christ is being eaten alive by gossip and slander among its members. I wish I could claim innocence in this area, but I know some middle-school girls who demonstrate more maturity and restraint with their tongues than I do. One of my greatest difficulties lies in the fact that I do not always know what gossip is, and what it is not. Webster defines gossip as "idle talk" and slander as malicious "defamation." Lately, I have tried to ask myself if what I am about to say is necessary and important, or if it is just idle chatter. I am more prone to slander someone behind their back when I am afraid of confronting them. If I do find the guts to confront them in person, then I feel less compulsion to tell others about the problem. Gossip is a symptom of boredom. If I am headed in an exciting direction and have my thoughts directed towards what comes next, why would I waste time knocking someone else's life? Those of us prone to gossip need to examine our hearts to discover what we gain from tearing others down.

Dealing with conflict is inevitable in all relationships, but it is important to balance rebuking sin with overlooking the faults of others. If faults need addressing then do so with bold humility; however be sure that you are truly trying to eliminate sin and not a person's individuality. I am still learning the difference between confronting wrongdoing and accepting a person with their faults. At times, I have not said enough and let anger and bitterness swell in its place. Other times, I have said too much and crushed a spirit. Focus your efforts on reminding people of their kingdom identity and you will have less energy to consider their faults.

It is easy to become frustrated in the pursuit of enduring friendships. I think few people have lifelong friends. Most of us have close friends for just a season. This is not a bad thing, for God will bring different people into our lives for different reasons. If God seems to keep putting the same type of person in your path, it may be wise to ask Him the reason. Is there something specific He is trying to teach you? Over the years, several of my close friends have demonstrated strong personalities and the ability to deal with conflict in a loving but firm manner. I believe one of the things God was trying to accomplish in my life through such friendships was to teach me how to confront difficult people and situations. I had a front row seat as my best friends modeled the very behavior that God was

Chapter Four – Friends

trying to teach me. What is He trying to teach you through your friends?

It is important to understand that your friends are in various stages of growth in their lives, and they will frequently disappoint you and fail to meet your expectations. This is why forgiveness is so important in all of our relationships. Resentment is a heavy weight on our hearts. It will consume us and sabotage our reputations if we let it. And it certainly does not make us more attractive to the opposite sex. Martin Luther said, "Stick with love. Hate is too great a burden to bear." He was right. Prolonged bitterness is a load our hearts were never made to carry. Let go and love, and notice how it lightens your heart.

One final word of wisdom: healthy friendships with former boyfriends or girlfriends are extremely rare. I will not say that they do not exist, but they are usually not the best for both parties. Do not be fooled. The two of you broke up for a reason and usually one or the other still hurts. To playact a friendship when so much has gone unsaid is not a friendship, but a charade.

THUMBS-UP

My church recently organized small groups to watch movies on a regularly scheduled weeknight. It was an opportunity to build community within the church, meet new people, and catch a flick related to the previous Sunday's sermon. Several groups were organized throughout the city and members opened up their homes. For many of the folks in my church, these movie nights were the start of some great friendships and a way for others to get plugged into the body.

Although I agreed that the movie nights were a great opportunity to build relationships within the church, I was hesitant to participate. None of my other single friends had signed up, and I did not know any of the families hosting the groups. Why would I want to hang out with a bunch of random people with whom I had nothing in common? Surely if I want to find a mate I should go to a bar, a club, or anywhere there are singles.

In the end I agreed to join a group that met across town. I decided to jump in with both feet. Though I knew none of the people in the group, I made it a point to get to know them. At first there seemed little to gain. Our group included Susan who was divorced, Diane who had been single all of her forty-five years, Ed who was a widower, Matt and Michelle who had been married for twenty-five years and had no children, and Mike and Emily who got married in their thirties and recently had their first child. And then there was me, the youngest in the group, single, and still not quite sure why I was there.

As we rolled the film for the evening I found myself looking around the room at each face. *How did these people get here? What has life been like for them?* I wondered how Susan felt when her marriage fell apart. Did it permanently shatter her dreams for romance? I wondered how many nights Diane had cried herself to sleep because years had passed and she was still alone. What kind of thoughts ran through Ed's mind after he lost his wife? What do you do when you are fifty-nine and single again? I doubt you go back to the club scene. Was it a source of great pain to Matt and Michelle knowing they would never have children or grand-children to spoil in their retirement years? How about Mike and Emily - how did they find each other after waiting so long?

Chapter Four – Friends

I also wondered what the group thought of me. Were they trying to figure out why I was not married? Did they wonder if something was wrong with me?

This was the motley group that met every other Thursday night to discuss a movie and its relevance for our lives. Several times I planned on not returning to the group, thinking I had nothing in common with these people. Yet, when Thursday night approached, I felt the need to go back. I do not know why I took time out of a busy schedule to go to my movie group, but I sensed it was important.

It was only after the movie series ended, and I had time to reflect on the group, that I realized what had transpired. This strange collection of people with diverse backgrounds, life experiences, marital statuses, and stages of life had become the body of Christ to each other. As the film credits rolled across the screen each week, and we began to discuss its message, slowly and steadily we began to share our lives with each other. Ed talked about how hard it was to work after his wife died. Susan talked about the pain of her divorce. Matt and Michelle shared the plans they were making for their retirement without children. Diane taught us what she had learned from being single for so many years. Mike and Emily confided how tight their finances were with the birth of their baby. I tend to pull the drawbridge up on my heart when I am with strangers, but I revealed my desire to find a spouse and admitted I was lonely.

The group listened carefully and tenderly to each of its members. We encouraged one another and reminded each other of God's promises. Ultimately, it was a safe place to share the hard stuff about our lives, and acknowledge how we desperately needed God's strength to carry us each day.

We had become the body of Christ to each other. The eye was helping the foot to see where to step. The ear was telling the nose what it heard. The hand was bringing food to the mouth. None of the people in my group were famous, wealthy, or powerful, but we were all children of the Father caught in a dark world where the only way to get through is by leaning on God and each other. Life had taken unexpected turns for each of us; none of us were sure what tomorrow would bring. But openness with each other was making the journey easier. A deep peace that passes understanding made us more alike on the inside than we were different on the outside.

Singles make a crippling mistake when they isolate themselves from the larger church body. I strongly support a church's specific ministry to its singles, but it must never be at the expense of fellowship with the larger body. If singles are not connected to families within the church, they will probably lose their peer group once they get married. Just try talking about your marriage struggles with your unmarried friends. Do you think they will really appreciate the discussion?

Paul used the analogy of the body to explain to the Corinthians how each part of the body of Christ needs each other. My guess is that if he had more time he would have told the Corinthians to particularly treasure their singles because they are the thumbs on the body of Christ. Your thumb on each hand is different than the other four fingers - it is versatile, strong, flexible, and indispensable. Try picking up the simplest of objects without using your thumbs. It can be pretty difficult. Thumbs are the only extremities that have their own wrestling league and can get you a ride to another city.

Singles are like thumbs on the body of Christ because they bring a versatility, dexterity, and individuality that the other members do not have. Passionate singles are living reminders to married folks that the goal of a life is not to get married, but rather to live each day to the fullest for the glory of God. Singles bring dexterity to the body because their skill and innovation keep the families of the church from falling into ruts and dry routines. God loves to use singles to build His kingdom because He knows He will enjoy a lot of one on one time with them along the way. A church without singles is like a body without thumbs.

The implications of our role in the body are huge. Often singles get neglected in the church or patronized by the married crowd because of their marital status. Often their schedules and resources are treated with less respect or they get passed over for any significant role in leadership. "I feel forgotten by the church" one single told me. It is important that churches appreciate the unique journey singles are taking and come alongside them to comfort them, encourage them, and invite them to find their particular role. I do not know any singles who will refuse a dinner invitation to a family's home, but I do know a lot of singles who become highly motivated when they are affirmed, comforted, and well fed.

The responsibility is also on us as singles to give our best to the body. Too often singles are guilty of moaning about the lack of invitations by families to get involved. Make the married crowd pay attention to you. Bring your "A" game to the church and they will stand up and notice you. Share your gifts with others and you will be surprised how quickly they pull up a chair for you. If you think that married couples do not want singles around, then think again. A husband told me recently that he and his wife prefer to befriend singles because it is too difficult to find another married couple in which all four people truly like each other. It is easier for the two of them to both like the same single.

Drop the church hop and take your place as a thumb on the body of Christ. Stop treating local churches the same as you do local bars. Go to the church where God calls you and bring the full measure of your glory to bear on that congregation. Live free and love radically, and people will take notice. If they are tempted to envy your passion, liberty, and dexterity, then you are a thumb doing its job. By the way, singles of kindred heart will meet you there, and they will be the kind of friends that *will* be there for you.

****

I first saw the movie *Under the Tuscan Sun* at exactly the right time. Its plot and message seemed to correspond in so many ways to my own life. It deals with the question of what to do when our dreams of love are unfulfilled. Where do we go when "happily ever after" seems so far away?

Frances is a well-known book critic and an aspiring author living in California. In the opening scene her heart is shattered when she learns of her husband's infidelity. Wallowing in grief, she struggles to make sense of her life. Finally her friend scares her into the realization that she is in danger of becoming "one of those people who just look like a shell of a person," and you wonder what in the world happened to them.

Frances admits she is afraid of never recovering from the divorce, so she does something radical. On a tour of Tuscany, Italy she spontaneously decides to buy an old house that needs a lot of work. She spends the next several months overseeing its remodeling, picking olives, and learning how to cook Italian. She also meets plenty of the locals, including two teenagers in love, her Polish contractors, and a crazy blonde who becomes her mentor. As the film develops we can tell that the house essentially becomes a metaphor for her heart and life. As she tackles one remodeling project after another, she is also forced to confront her anger, fear, and loneliness. More than anything, including a great house in Tuscany, Frances longs for a husband and a family.

A key scene in the film is when a promising romance ends and Frances is left crushed again. Her dreams for love seem farther away than ever. She begins smashing things in her bedroom, collapses in tears, and cries out in utter frustration, "What can I do?"

What happens next is amazing. Instead of retreating into self-pity and fear Frances chooses to connect again. She helps teenage lovers secure the blessing of a father. While everything is screaming to the contrary within her, she tells them the importance of believing in true love. She reaches out to help her friend who has unexpectedly become a single mother. She continues to wave to a neighbor every morning who never waves back. At the end of the story, she does find a lover, but only after she has opened up her new home to the entire village to celebrate the lives of others. In her decision to connect, give, reach out, and love when all the pain and fear from her past tells her not to, she becomes irresistibly attractive to her friends and her long awaited love.

What a great picture for those of us who are still waiting for a spouse. There is no better way to spend our time as singles than with hearts full of compassion and love for others. Not surprisingly, when we strive to love others well, we will find the love we have been looking for all along.

The Single Journey

CHAPTER FIVE

MENTORS

Friendship is seldom lasting but between equals, or where the superiority on one side is reduced by some equivalent advantage on the other.
- Samuel Johnson

Be imitators of me, as I am of Christ.
- (I Corinthians 11:1; ESV)

Wisdom has built her spacious house with seven pillars. She has prepared a great banquet, mixed the wines, and set the table. She has sent her servants to invite everyone to come. She calls out from the heights overlooking the city. 'Come home with me,' she urges the simple. To those without good judgment, she says, 'Come, eat my food, and drink the wine I have mixed. Leave your foolish ways behind, and begin to live; learn how to be wise.'
- (Proverbs 9:1-6)

There are only a few movies that I can watch over and over. Most of the time I am like everybody else - when I want to catch a flick on a Friday night, I want to watch a new release. There is, however, a handful of movies that I never tire of seeing again and again. You probably have your own list of favorites that you keep watching as well. *Spy Game* is one of these movies for me. Regardless of how many times I watch it, I never get bored and I catch something new every time.

In case you missed this movie, *Spy Game* is about the relationship between a veteran CIA agent named Nathan Muir (Robert Redford) and a younger agent whom he personally trains, named Tom Bishop (Brad Pitt). As the film develops so does their relationship. We learn that they first met in Vietnam when Muir recruited Bishop as a sniper. The veteran was so impressed with the youth that he took him under his wing and trained him personally. Over the course of the movie he teaches him how to make a contact, how to recruit an asset, and how to solicit information from a complete stranger. Muir makes sure that Bishop knows the latest technology and learns the best survival skills. Together they work dangerous OPs (Special Operations) in Vietnam, Cold War Berlin, and war torn Beirut. Conflict, respect, and teamwork characterize their relationship. They often disagree on methods, but they somehow work together to achieve one objective after another.

The story of their relationship is told against the background of a crisis. An OP goes bad and Bishop is being held in a Chinese prison. In twenty-four hours he will be executed by the Chinese government on the charge of espionage. The film is a race against the clock. As Muir tells the story of his relationship with his apprentice, he is rushing around CIA headquarters seeking Bishop's release. The veteran agent summons his best efforts to

Chapter Five – Mentors

overcome the bureaucracy of the Agency, the indifference of his superiors, and the ticking of the clock. All this on his last day as an agent before retirement. Bishop's freedom is secured in the end, but not before Muir has given up his life's savings and risked his professional reputation by breaking all kinds of Agency rules. The final scene shows Bishop being hustled out of China on a helicopter realizing that it was his mentor, his advisor, his friend that won him his freedom.

The reason I am so drawn to this film is because of the relationship between these two men. I admire their individual strength and how they strengthen each other. I am grabbed by the invitation the veteran offers the youth to experience a new and larger life, a life that is dangerous, exciting, but also significant. The younger man receives the personal time and attention of the older man. Lessons that took the veteran a lifetime to learn are offered unreservedly to the apprentice. Weaknesses and mistakes are confronted. What begins as a job for the government becomes a committed relationship. Even when the mentored one walks away from the mentor, the veteran does not flinch in his commitment to his pupil. They have been through too much together. They have become too close to forget each other. In the end, the older one gives up everything for the life of the younger.

After watching the film, I knew what was missing in my life. I wanted a veteran agent to teach me combat and survival skills, not so I could live in the forest, but so I could live in this world. I wanted someone who would share a lifetime of knowledge and experiences with me - someone who would teach me what it truly means to live as a son of the Great King and how to fight against the realms of darkness. I wanted personal training. I wanted a mentor.

CLUELESS

One of my greatest fears as a single male, who longs to be married, is that slowly and steadily I will become "unmarriable." What I mean is that gradually over time, without a wife who keeps me from wearing suspenders with a belt, or chides me when I drink milk straight from the container, I will develop habits and patterns that become a turn-off to women. I fear that I will begin to act, talk, look, dress, smell, and live like a bachelor rather than as a guy who happens to be single. My female readers probably know exactly what I mean because you have met many of these men. However, some of my slower male readers may not be following this, so let me give the clueless bachelors an example.

About a year ago I had lunch with a guy, who I will call Jack, at a local fast-food chain. Jack and I were both in graduate school at the time, and decided to grab a quick meal before getting back to class. Stepping up to the counter Jack placed his order first. That is, he finally placed his order after discussing out loud the pros and cons of ordering each combo meal. He wanted a super-sized soda, but did not like the fact that the burger would be one-half pound of meat with onions. You see, he did not like the taste of a lot of red meat and onions. Of course he could order the chicken sandwich, but he preferred to eat chicken with a special honey mustard sauce of which they were all out. The endless menu wrangling continued as a growing line of people behind me became more irate. The teenage girl working the cash register looked like a cast member of the Real World and kept playing with her hoop earrings as she waited for Jack to make his decision. Finally, he chose Combo Meal #4... no, #3... no, #5 without onions and paid for his meal. When it was finally my turn to order, I just asked for Combo Meal #1 as fast as I could. I had no clue what I was ordering; I just wanted to hurry so that the people behind me would not hurt me.

I made the mistake of asking Jack where he wanted to sit. "In a booth, there's always more room," he replied. I started carrying my tray of food to a booth, but then he said if we sat near the window we could watch the people walk by. I reversed direction and headed towards the window. Of course he did not want to be in the sun, so he suggested we sit at a table. I spun on one heel back toward the tables. Then he noted we could always eat at one of the tables outside in the shade - I started walking towards the left. Then again we could always take our food back to the campus and eat it there - I started walking to the right. "Nah, let's just eat in a booth," he decided. I did one more 360 and landed in a booth. It took only a minute and half for Jack to decide where to eat, and in the same time I had performed a new line dance for everyone in the restaurant.

As I ate my now cold Combo Meal #1, I listened to Jack discuss everything from the theological ramifications of Eastern Orthodox ecclesiology to the reason why women should want him regardless of how he looked. He felt that any opinions regarding his physical appearance were just erratic emotions. As Jack continued to talk, I wondered if the ketchup and the mayonnaise were competing against each other to see which could make the most spots on Jack's t-shirt. Mayonnaise led ketchup for most of the meal, but on the last handful of French fries, yes handful, ketchup took the checkered flag.

Alright, maybe I exaggerated one or two details about Jack, but I do distinctly remember walking away from the table thinking, "I need to hurry up and get married so that my wife will nag me away from complacency." We guys tend to get set in our ways as we get older, unless there's a woman around to make us buy new socks. Of course we males are not alone in this department. Women buy new socks whether or not they are married, but it seems that age takes its toll on them as well, as they become more controlling and harried as the years pass without a ring.

Martin Luther referred to marriage as the school for character and believed it was superior to the monastery for sanctifying a soul. A friend told me recently that when he got married he felt like a giant mirror had been dropped in front of him, and he saw his true character for the first time. Living that close to someone else requires a pattern of confession and seeking forgiveness unlike any other. As painful as it sometimes will be, I look forward to having a wife that will call me on my sin and point me in the direction of repentance and change.

But what about now? What can single men do when there is no wife to tell them to stop spitting in the kitchen sink? What can single women do when there is no husband to encourage them to forgive their partner at work? How do you tell somebody what they need to change if everyone else is afraid to bring it up? Who will you allow to examine your life so that you won't become more and more unattractive and "unmarriable"?

Singles often neglect a very valuable resource for answering these questions. A healthy relationship with a mentor is one of the best ways to keep singles on their toes: physically, mentally, socially, and spiritually. Family and friends may have a tendency to leave us where we are in our growth. More often than not, they may not be able to see who we could become with a little truth and encouragement. It is unlikely that they will point out fears, ways we avoid intimacy, or habits that make us difficult to be around.

Chapter Five – Mentors

Whose voice will speak this kind of truth into your life? A mentor who is experienced with life, has fought for his or her own heart, who speaks the truth boldly, and who wants the best for you can serve as this voice. Otherwise, singles of both genders run the risk of getting stuck in deep ruts.

There is no ten-step process that I can outline to tell you how to establish and execute a mentoring relationship. It is a relationship that is built over time, probably unexpectedly, and is based on truth, trust, commitment, and openness. What I can do for you is share a little about my relationship with Larry, who began mentoring me three years ago. I hope by giving you a peek at my mentor, you will have a better idea of what to look for as you seek someone who is a veteran at living life.

WHO IS THIS GUY?

I first met Larry when I was a high school teacher. That day began in the usual manner of eating the same bland cereal, wearing one of the usual shirts and ties, and dragging myself to a classroom full of adolescents at an hour too early for all of us. I rummaged through the piles of debris on my desk looking for some lifeless worksheet. I figured I would keep my students busy during the first hour as I pulled myself together for the day ahead.

As I was doing my best to look organized and prepared for another day of learning, I heard a knock at the door. Frustrated with the interruption, I flung open the door and with forced courtesy asked, "Can I help you?"

Before me stood a tall, broad-shouldered guy with long hair and an earring. Wearing a polo shirt, jeans, and cowboy boots he looked like a cross between a Hell's Angel and an American cowboy. I was not sure if I should call for help or refer him to the bar down the street, but I was quite certain he was in the wrong place. Yet, he had kind eyes and asked rather politely, "Is this room #102?"

"Ah, yes it is," I replied with some reservation.

"Oh, great. I'm Larry, you know - Nick's dad." I spun the rolodex of student names in my head and then remembered Nick in my third period class. He was a great kid who I respected. How could this be his dad?

"Oh, right. I know Nick," I said trying to figure out what was going on.

"The office assigned me to this room for the first half of the period. You get to go to the café for a free breakfast since it's Teacher Appreciation Week," he said.

I stood there for a moment, trying to figure out how this guy could be Nick's dad. What he was saying was true; it was Friday and the faculty was getting a free breakfast while approved parents watched their classes. Maybe somebody failed to run a background check on this guy, but a free breakfast and a break from the kids sounded pretty good to me.

"Oh yeah, you're right," I said. "Well they have an assignment, so just make sure they complete the worksheet and, well, make sure they keep my classroom in one piece." Larry nodded as I walked out of the room. I laughed to myself thinking he was just like most parents who think teaching is easy until they actually get in the classroom. *This class period will be a waste,* I thought to myself. But at least I would get a good breakfast.

Chapter Five – Mentors

I sat in the café for several minutes, eating cold waffles and wondering what was going on in my classroom. Would Larry have the guts to keep the students in line? Was he qualified to answer questions about the lesson? I envisioned my classroom being torn apart by my students, and my well-intentioned substitute cringing fearfully in the corner. I was sure my precious bulletin boards would be destroyed, every grade changed in my grade book, and my computer thrown out the window by the time I got back. I had never met a parent before that knew what to do with a room full of teenagers. This one would be no different.

I could have sat in the café for a full half hour, but after twenty minutes my nerves got the better of me, and I headed back to my class to rescue Larry from an early demise. By the time I reached my room I was expecting the worse, but when I walked through the door I could not believe my eyes.

There were 25 of the rowdiest teenagers sitting motionless at their desks, transfixed on the figure standing before them, hanging on every word. No one dared interrupt. They were mesmerized.

As I listened, Larry's words poured out like water on parched souls. He told them story after story about people he had met in his counseling practice, in the wilderness, or in the business world. He talked to the kids honestly and sincerely about alcohol, friends, eating disorders, sex, college, romance, and God. He drew diagrams on the board to help communicate his ideas. He shared his own heart. He asked the students for feedback and then guided their responses towards wisdom. I had never seen my students so gripped – not even on my best days. Larry stopped when he finally saw me at the door and said, "Oh, you're back. Do you want me to stop?"

I did not even think about saying yes. Not even for a moment. Not only would I have had a riot on my hands, but I, too, was caught under Larry's spell. I wanted to hear more, so I took a seat in the back and began to learn from the man who would come to teach me so much in the future. All the time I listened I kept wondering, "Who is this guy that speaks so brilliantly to hearts?"

When the class was over I begged him to come back for my third period class. "You have to! You were great! They loved it! *I* loved it!" At this point, it was more for me than my students. He said he had to check his schedule, but would do his best to come back for third period. And when he did, another whole class loved him again. As the bell rang and the students left, I went up to him and said, "That was great! They were really listening! How do you do that? What did you mean when you said…? Did you ever consider being a teacher? What kind of music do you listen to? What football team do you cheer for? Oh, and by the way, who are you?"

Thus began my friendship with Larry who would become my mentor, my advisor, my fishing guide, my spiritual father, my partner, and most of all my friend. He means a great deal to me; I would not be the man I am today without him.

WILD

Perhaps the most intriguing facet about my relationship with Larry is that we are nothing alike. In fact, if you knew each of us you would never put us together. We do not look the same, dress the same, talk the same, or have the same interests. Larry loves to hunt. I do not. I love scuba diving. Larry does not. He loves the forest. I love the beach. We read different

Chapter Five – Mentors

books, have different friends, go to different churches, and cheer for different teams. On the surface it would seem that we have absolutely nothing in common.

Yet I believe this is the great strength of our relationship. If Larry and I were exactly alike how could he take me to new places? The reason Larry can lead me to new levels of growth is because he shows me a different way to see life. What would be the point of his mentoring if he simply agreed with me and kept me where I was? Moreover, Larry has never tried to make me like himself. He has always respected and promoted my individuality, and has acknowledged that his opinion is not the only way. I do not want to be Larry. I want to be Pete. Larry helps me be who I truly am as Pete.

Larry exercises great wisdom in leading me to new places. It is probably his wildness to which I am most attracted. At times, he has asked me uncomfortable questions that I did not want to answer. Other times, he has pointed out errors in my thinking, particularly lies about myself. Sometimes, he has told me the truth and I have disliked him for it. Other times, he has met me in my fear and encouraged me to get back into the game. It is not uncommon for him to just listen and acknowledge my pain. When he prays for me I am reassured and know everything will be okay.

Openness is a key feature in our relationship. It is important that I know I can talk to him about anything and not be laughed at or dismissed. I can be transparent with him because he is transparent with me. He does not set himself above me, but rather is quick to tell me about his struggles. In other words, none of his identity is tied into being my mentor, so he is free to love me well.

There are very few grown men who are strong enough to express their love for another brother. Too often guys are so busy trying to look macho that they think needing or wanting male companionship is a sign of weakness. Actually the opposite is true. Larry exhibits great strength because he loves other men well. He affirms their masculinity, validates their importance, and calls out their strength. As the recipient of such masculine love, I am a better man because of it. I have met far too many single men who cannot communicate, cannot express need, are afraid of dreaming big, cannot admit failure, and are consequently very weak. The most important lesson Larry has taught me, through his actions rather than his words, is that sanctification includes a growing inner strength. My great prayer for my single male readers is that God would increase their inner strength whereby they will share their hearts boldly, sacrifice for their women, and learn to love other men well. Paul prayed the same way for the Ephesians (Eph. 3:16).

I cannot say what a mentoring relationship would look like between two women, but I imagine it would be similar. If it is the male mentor's job to draw out the strength of another man, then it is the call of a female mentor to draw out the beauty of a younger woman's heart. Is she living in fear rather than freedom? Does she deprive the world of her glorious femininity? Does she tend to cling to men or to control them? My friend, Amy, told me that if not for her mentor, she would have slipped back into the shadowy fears and self-defeat of her past. Her mentor believes in her, reminds her who she is, *whose* she is, and who she is becoming. Their relationship is a great portrait of two women sharing life together.

It might be helpful for you to know that Larry and I have never formalized any kind of mentoring agreement between us. We did not sign a contract outlining the responsibilities of each party, neither did we go through some kind of ceremony, ritual, or rite. Our relationship developed naturally. In fact, the word mentor is rarely used when we mention each other. Rather, he refers to me as his partner, friend, and son. The healthiest mentoring relationships are ones where the line between the mentor and the mentored one becomes blurred. Gradually the two of you become close friends. A person who is truly experienced with life will demonstrate his character by proving he is not above developing intimacy with someone less experienced. Again, it is strength, not weakness, to be open to learn anything from anybody. That is why I refer to Larry as my friend rather than as my mentor.

I realize that what I have with Larry is unique. God may not bring the same type of relationship into your life. There is great diversity within the body of Christ, and God has many paths for getting you where He wants you to go. Mentoring is just one of those paths. It may help to remember the following points as you seek out a mentor.

Your mentor does not have to be the sole definitive voice of truth in your life. In fact, I would advise against this. There are several people in my life who have encouraged or convicted me at the proper time. My friend, Brent, has comforted me several times in my loneliness. Louise, a wife of 23 years and mother of three great kids, has changed my life for the better with her rich counsel and wisdom.

God may provide you with one mentor for the course of your life, or with different mentors for life's various seasons. You may need to pursue them, but if they want the relationship as well, they will consistently respond to your pursuit. These are not accountability partners to whom you report each week how much you have sinned and get a "do better next time" talk.

These are first and foremost relationships where conversations about sports, national events, or work naturally develop into conversations about life, love, and truth. Your mentor must have the courage to ask you tough questions and firmly proclaim the truth; you must have the courage to face examination and correction. You will not agree on everything, but that is alright. Again, your goal is not to become your mentor. Your quest is to become you like never before. Your mentor offers you his or her experiences to help you along the way.

Looking to an experienced mentor can be an exciting way to enrich your life during your single years and beyond. Perhaps as equally maturing can be your relationships with younger men or women whom you mentor. Some of the best mentoring you can receive for your life will occur as you mentor others. Singles who refuse to be mentored refuse to be known, and establish a headstrong spirit that will only hold them back in life. Ask God to give you a wise mentor for your single journey. It may not be who you expect, but by God's great wisdom it will be who you need.

A DOUBLE PORTION

I cannot imagine what it must have been like to be Elisha. He was a great man of God, but he followed in the footsteps of the famous prophet Elijah. This was no small legacy to carry forward. Elijah was the founder of the school of the prophets. He had predicted a prolonged drought in Israel, and when it occurred, he was miraculously fed by ravens in the wilderness. He single-handedly took on all the priests of Baal at Mount Carmel and won. Several times he called down fire from heaven to consume a sacrifice or entire armies. He went head-to-head against the evil king, Ahab, and did not back down. He was one of the greatest heroes in the history of God's kingdom.

In his final hours, he appointed his assistant, Elisha, as his successor. Elisha was to continue the great prophet's ministry and proclaim truth and righteousness in Israel. Together Elijah and Elisha spent these last hours together traveling through the cities of the kingdom. The younger prophet learned much from his mentor, but soon he would be on his own. He refused to be separated from the old man in the final hours. His heart was bound to him and he listened only closer in their final moments together. Before leaving, the old prophet turned to his apprentice and successor and asked, "What shall I do for you, before I am taken from you?"

Elisha answered without hesitation. "Please let there be a double portion of your spirit on me." The old prophet could see the zeal in his successor's eyes - the passion, the fire, and the ignorance of youth. He, too, once had those same eyes, but now he had entered the winter of his life. In a moment he would be transported to glory, sidestepping the grave. His apprentice would be left behind, alone. Had he taught Elisha well? Would he be faithful? Only the years ahead would reveal the answer.

Elisha's request would only be granted if he saw Elijah being taken up to heaven. Had God heard his plea? The answer was not long in coming. Suddenly a blazing chariot, pulled by horses, descended and separated Elisha from his mentor. The heat of the flames was more intense than anything he had ever felt; yet, he was not burned. By the time he pulled his hand away from his face his beloved mentor was gone. The old prophet had been taken to glory and Elisha cried out, "My father, my father! The chariots of Israel and its horsemen!"

All that remained was the old and tattered cloak of Elijah. Holding back the tears from losing the man who had taught him so much, Elisha tore his own clothes and picked up the cloak of the great prophet. Immediately, he was filled with the Spirit of God. The waters of the Jordan separated before him allowing him to pass. The other prophets acknowledged his authority. In the years to come Elisha would perform miracles and fight battles just as significant as his mentor. Miraculous feedings, raising the dead, and blinding entire armies became part of his resume. Indeed, a double portion of the spirit of Elijah had come to rest upon Elisha. The old prophet had departed, but his work and legacy lived on in the life he had mentored.

CHAPTER SIX

DATING

This swift business / I must uneasy make, lest too light winning / Make the prize light.
                                         - William Shakespeare

Anyone who does not love does not know God – for God is love.
                                         - (I John 4:8)

  The only prayer request I make more frequently than my desire for a spouse, is my desire for a nice green lawn. If I prayed for missionaries as much as I pray for green grass, then all of Africa and Asia would be converted by now. I have told God on many occasions that if He is not going to give me a wife, He should at least give me a nice lawn. Right now my lawn looks like a hay field, so God knows He will continue to hear from me.

  Meanwhile, I continue to receive unsolicited advice regarding my hapless lawn. It is rather strange how as soon as people hear you are having lawn troubles, they feel compelled to tell you what to do. I have patiently listened to story after story of what people have done with their lawns and how lush and green they look now. They always conclude their story with strong advice regarding the course I should take with my lawn.

I have been told to mow the grass higher and mow the grass lower. I have been told to water it twice a week for 15 minute intervals, and I have been told to water it every day for a half hour. I have been told to fertilize it twice each year, and others have said once a month. Some have advised to fill in the bare spots with plugs, others have recommended sod. Still others say grass seed is the best. At present count, three different pesticides have been pushed my way as well as different products to make the grass greener. Alas, after months of planting, digging, trimming, cutting, killing, feeding, nurturing, and praying my front lawn still looks like it has been struck by a nuclear winter. I am planning to have a load of sand dumped over everything to solve the problem. Then, if I try to sell my house, I can advertise it as a beach house.

My lawn is a lot like my love life. I get a lot of unwanted advice and experience mostly frustration as a result. The same well-intentioned folks that try to rescue my lawn also try to rescue my dating life. Why are you not married yet? Don't you want to be married? I am told to go out more and meet more people, go to more clubs, bars, bookstores, and restaurants. I am told to meet people at concerts, sporting events, or comedy clubs, to go back to school and meet other students. Others say I should wait on God and stay home - God will bring me the right one, so I don't need to do anything about it. Others tell me to change churches and go where there are plenty of singles. I have been told I am too aggressive and too passive, too much in a rush and too slow. I should try online dating, speed dating, video dating, phone dating, and even reality TV dating.

Chapter Six – Dating

I have been told I should date only women who are older and only women who are younger. I should be more narrow in who I date. I should be more open in who I date. Focus more on attraction. Focus less on attraction. I should date someone who is the opposite of me. I should date someone who is just like me. Date good girls. Date bad girls. Missionary date. Date friends. Date blind.

If I am not married yet it is because my self-esteem is too low. I need to affirm myself more, express myself, center myself, forgive myself, and know myself. I should be more humble. I should be bolder. I should ask more, flirt more, talk more, spend more, read more, and call more. Or I should ask less, flirt less, talk less, spend less, read less, and call less.

What about her? Why don't you ask her out? I'm too fussy, too picky, too reckless or too accepting, too open, and too cautious. I'll never know when God will bring me the one, but at the same time I am supposed to know when she is the one. There is supposed to be more than one person I can marry, but I am also told to wait for the perfect match. I once read a book that recommended polygamy as a way to relieve the pressure of finding just the right one.

All this competing and conflicting advice makes me feel like an operator at a switchboard trying to manage over one hundred irate callers at the same time. No wonder dating can be such a frustrating topic for singles to discuss! Many of them do not even want to admit that they are single.

A friend of mine was planning to have me speak at his church singles group in town. But when he told the group that a friend was coming to speak, who was also writing a book on singleness, they all groaned! They did not even know my name,

107

who I was, or what I was going to say, but they did not want any more talks on singleness.

In light of the verbal diarrhea you have probably received with dating advice, I have no intention of offering you more. It is unfortunate that Christians have followed in the footsteps of the world by trying to find the best formula for dating success. A strategy or procedure may help you meet your goal of marriage, but it will deprive you of a lot of growth and excitement along the way. Rather, what I hope to give you in this chapter is some insight into your heart regarding dating. I also want to show you how tips and techniques fall short of what Jesus offers. My words will not answer your who, what, where, and when questions about dating, but hopefully they will restore some of the mystery, adventure, and romance that has been lost in this area of our lives.

PRODIGALS AND PHARISEES

Jesus must have been a master storyteller. People were willing to sit for hours in the hot sun just to listen to Him. Sometimes they would go without food all day so they would not lose their seat close to Him. They would follow Him wherever He went, mob Him with their sick relatives, and even rip the roofs off of houses to reach Him. No doubt His miracles and divine teaching were a big draw, but so were His stories. He had an incredible ability to keep your attention with realistic characters, vivid imagery, and plot lines you could appreciate. In my opinion, the best story He ever told was the story of the Prodigal Son.

The story is one of the classics in the Bible, but perhaps it has been misnamed; a better title would have been the Story

Chapter Six – Dating

of the Two Sons. After all, Jesus begins the parable with the remark, "There was a man who had two sons." This is a fitting way to begin the story because we soon learn the two sons take opposite paths in life.

The younger son, as you may recall, demands his share of the inheritance early from his father and goes off to a far country to squander his wealth with thieves and prostitutes. Only when he becomes utterly desperate does he decide to return home and beg his father to hire him as a servant. Of course the father dismisses the suggestion, embraces his prodigal son, clothes him, and throws a big party to celebrate his return. All this happens to the consternation of the pharisaical older brother. He has always been responsible and followed the rules, never asking his father even for a young goat to eat with his friends. He refuses to go inside the house to celebrate his brother's return. In the end the father pleads with the older son to join the party, and reminds him that all that he has is his. They must celebrate because his brother was dead, but is now alive. He was lost, but is now found.

This particular parable of Jesus fascinates me. Each of the brothers capture two different types of people. Prodigals are the folks in the world or church who live life on the wild side. They may be fun and exciting to be around, but they can also be reckless, directionless, and dishonest. Rules are made to be broken. When they sin, they sin well. When they jump, they jump headfirst. They often leave a wake of wreckage behind them.

Pharisees on the other hand are like the older brother in the parable. They never step out of line because they are trying to do life the "right way." They live by the book, color inside the lines, and never speak out of turn. They know the rules, follow the rules, and throw the rules in everybody else's face. They demand predictable results. If anyone is having a good time it is probably because they are being "worldly." They know they are doing life correctly compared to the people around them who are blowing it. Good thing they are not like them.

The world tends to be full of prodigals who ignore the rules and ask questions later. The church tends to be full of Pharisees who try to feel good about themselves by pointing out how far ahead they are of the ungodly. Both prodigals and Pharisees, however, are found in the church and world, and nowhere are these two types better revealed than when it comes to dating.

THE ODD COUPLES

What happens when prodigals go on dates? How about Pharisees? If you do not think you are a Pharisee or a prodigal then I regret to inform you that everyone leans in one direction or the other. Even the most sincere Christians will oscillate between license and legalism. Moreover, you will reveal your inclination in the way you date. Allow me to illustrate.

When it comes right down to it prodigals just have fewer inhibitions on the dating scene. They are open to romance anytime, anywhere, with anybody. No list of "gotta-haves" is in their pocket. They are living life too fast to write things down. Bars, clubs, cybercafés, concerts, or personal ads are all just fine for meeting other people. They feel at ease in any setting because they have read all the latest literature on self-esteem boosting, self-image boosting, body boosting, conversation boosting, and attraction boosting. They know all the latest pick-

Chapter Six – Dating

up lines and have even invented a few themselves. (Can I check your shirt label to see if you were made in heaven?)

No conversations are off limits at dinner for prodigals including what their therapist told them that morning or how they would like to hex their ex. The touching, rubbing, massaging, tickling and goofy looks begin on the first date and only progress. Sometimes Saturday night dinner turns into Sunday morning breakfast, but it is okay when it is with someone "special" and "meant to be." Even though they are always breaking up, they stay in the game because nothing can stop the power of love.

Meanwhile there are always Pharisees close by, clicking their tongues at the prodigals. They specialize in doing things the right way and not messing up their lives. They are intent on avoiding worldliness. In fact, they belong to another world – the world three hundred years ago when carriages were considered rapid transit and ladies thought it an elite privilege to wear a corset. Not only are Pharisees holier than prodigals on a date, they are even too holy for a date. They prefer to call it courtship. Pharisees only go to restaurants with somebody of the opposite sex when all four parents - Uncle Bill, Aunt Rose, Cousin Tom, and Pastor Smith - accompany them. Heaven forbid unbridled passion is awakened and someone loses control. They must memorize Bible verses to keep them from lust and wear their purity ring as a reminder to avoid shaking hands. And if things really go too far physically then they can use their "Purity Quarter" to call a friend to come pick them up.

Fortunately their three accountability groups will stop them from defiling their sweetheart in their minds if they start becoming attracted. The best part is that when the day of their wedding arrives, they will have successfully withheld their touch from their partner, along with their dreams, fears, aspirations, struggles, hopes, desires and everything else that is a part of them. After all, guarding your heart means locking it up and throwing away the key, right?

Am I exaggerating these two types? Maybe, but not by much. All of us tend to lean in one of these two directions. Sometimes we can exhibit characteristics from both. It is wise for us to at least examine what we tend to do around the opposite sex. Are both styles completely bad? No. In fact, they both exhibit some strengths that I want to explore in this chapter. I just want to make the point that if you tend to date like a prodigal, then you are being reckless with your heart. If you use your heart to play badminton, then you will eventually miss and hit the ground. On the other hand, if you tend to be a Pharisee in your dating then realize that your self-righteousness is a sham. Even worse, you are being dishonest by focusing on rules and recipes rather than letting yourself be known. Recklessness *and* rules are both poor substitutes for the gift of relationship.

FOLLOW ME

What if? What if there was something better than license and legalism? What if you were able to enjoy the flow of the dance rather than counting time and watching your feet? What if your dating life had more excitement and drama than arranging your sock drawer? What if the rejoicing became greater than the recklessness and the passion greater than the procedure? I believe it is possible.

Most likely this is not the first book you have read on being single. In fact, you've probably scanned pages in the bookstore about how to find the perfect mate, how to do relationships correctly, or where to meet muscular men or buxom babes who love Jesus. So if you are standing in a bookstore reading this right now and have skipped to this page looking for a dating guide, then put the book back on the shelf. Go back to the fiction section because you have missed the entire point of this book. There is no formula for success, no flowchart of six easy steps for finding a mate, no recommendations on the best clubs in your city, and no recipe for avoiding a broken heart. There is no fool proof method for a single Christian to get married. But there is something better - a relationship with the person who said, "Follow me."

Why is it that Christians, who have the only religion in the world in which their God and Savior is also their friend, want to trade it in for a mechanical system of dos and don'ts? We secretly barter with God in the recesses of our heart that if we are good, do lots of Bible study, and follow God's rules then He will give us our dream mate. We are willing to bypass much growth and experience along the way. The stark truth is that God responds to such an offer with the words "no deal." God seems cruel at this point. Did we not hold up our end of the bargain? Are we not good little Christians who abstain from worldly enticements and color inside the lines? Perhaps, but God never wants to be part of such a deal. He wants so much more; of course we do too.

God wants to walk with His children through this life in an intimate and growing relationship. He wants to be in close conversation each day about what thrills us and what saddens us along the way. He wants to party with us, yet, we often choose to stay outside the house and grumble that we have slaved away for God, but He will not give us the one thing we ask for –a marriage partner. He invites us to be His children, but we insist on being His hired hands doing all kinds of Christian things for Him if He will just grant us our wages. God says, "No deal." He loves us too much to let us live in such slavery.

The only successful strategy for dating is to yield our hearts to Jesus' command: "Follow me." When we begin to follow, He will take us on an unusual path. This path will always lead in the direction of relationship – relationship with Him and relationships with others. The way will be unclear; it will take unexpected twists and turns. Sometimes, we will object to the terrain, and sometimes we will treasure the view, but it will be constantly evolving, developing, and full of surprises. That's what relationship is – a lot of the unexpected and uncontrollable. Anything else is mechanistic and quite frankly, not worth it.

When we take Jesus' words to follow Him seriously, then all of a sudden our dating life takes on a new flair. We become open to meeting new people. We let God surprise us through unexpected encounters. We learn to see every heart as a unique treasure waiting to be mined. We begin sharing our hearts, not tossing them around or locking them up, but letting people know who we are and what we dream about. Gradually we become open to spontaneity, aware of who we truly desire as a partner, and empowered to receive what God is giving us, shunning what He is refusing. In short, we know where we are going and who God wants to go with us.

There will be surprises along the way. Relationships we thought were made in heaven may end unexpectedly. People we never believed we could love may become our lifelong spouse. The joys and the sorrows along the way are God's way of awakening and maturing His children. The single question we need to ask along the way is, *"Where are we going now Lord?"*

He will not leave us hanging without an answer, and His answer will be good.

THE UNKNOWN

You have to admire Abraham. God commands him to leave his hometown and head towards an unknown place – and by the way, he will be blessed big time if he goes. That's it. That is all the information Abraham gets. As for me, I would have had a whole list of questions for God before I would up and leave my home. I would want to know how far the Promised Land was from the beach; how close was the nearest NASCAR track? Was there a good country music station in town? I would need these and other life essential questions answered before I obeyed God.

Apparently Abraham had more faith than I do because the Bible says he packed his wife, kids, and other relatives into the car and headed west even though he did not know where he was going. Because of his obedience, God blessed him abundantly in Canaan. In fact, He used Abraham's family to establish His kingdom people. The Son of God is also a descendant of father Abraham. The patriarch's willingness to walk into the unknown, alongside His God in intimate relationship, changed the world.

This is what my dating life needs. An intimate relationship with my Savior and friend who can help me chart these turbulent waters. I need an invitation from my loving Sovereign to step into the mysterious relationship that can occur between a man and a woman. I need the promise of my elder brother, Jesus, to never leave me or forsake me regardless of what happens in the plot. I need to be given the strength and faith to step into the unknown and unpredictable without hanging onto an obsession or strategy. I need the promise of blessing to know that it is not all in vain. I need relationship more than recklessness or rules. What does it mean to bring Jesus' words "follow me" to bear on my dating life? Volumes could be written to answer this question, but let me highlight six characteristics.

Rejoicing

Rejoicing should characterize my relationship with God. If following Christ is only duty and drudgery, then I will not last long. I am made to experience joy and I will perish if I do not. This aspect of my relationship with God is carried over to my dating life when I believe God is for me in my desire for the opposite sex. He is not sitting on His rocking chair in heaven groaning at my desire for love. He is not wondering when I am going to give up this silly notion of romance. He created sunsets for romantic walks, fire for candlelight dinners, and the moon for goodnight kisses. He smiles over my love for Valentine's Day cards, slow dances, and the smell of a perfumed woman. He is excited, even more than I am, when a woman says yes to dinner. He rejoices *over* me and rejoices *with* me.

This is very important for me to remember because I have not always thought this way. When I was a sophomore in college I believed God was only interested in me for what I could do for Him. I spent endless hours in college ministry and Bible study because I was sure these were the things that concerned God. Romance was a minor concession He might grant me if I was really good. But doing spiritual things was more important than the matters of my heart. As a result, I did not date at all that year, and went out little. If God wasn't interested, why bother? I won the Pharisee of the Year award and discovered how boring life can be when you are distant from God. What a shame that I wasted a full year of college doing religion rather than relationship.

Lamenting

As we walk through life with Jesus, rejoicing will not be our only experience. Lamenting will be an equally powerful expression of our relationship with Him. The road will get rough, the car will break down, there won't be any gas stations for miles, and it will begin to rain. In other words, we will go through tribulation. Not until heaven will all of our troubles be put behind us. In the meantime, He warned us this world is full of trouble, but to take heart for He has overcome the world. Therefore, all areas of our life, including dating, will cause heartache that drives us to cry out to the Father. Anyone who tries to sell you a system that delivers romance without frustration or pain is offering a sham. Even the best marriages face plenty of heartache. Crying out to God amidst the heartache is the path the heart in union with Christ chooses.

I dated a wonderful girl not too long ago. The relationship brought great joy to my life and I started to believe we would go the distance. Yet, when the relationship ended, I was sick with frustration and disappointment. I struggled with anger towards God. As I was driving home from our last time together I yelled out loud, "Why did you let this happen? Don't you understand? God where are you in all of this? Why have you abandoned me?" I had to pull the car over so I could say everything I wanted to say to Him. I really let Him have it. And you know what? He listened to every word. He was strong enough to bear my pain and had strength left over to hold me up. Lamenting the loss of someone important to me put words to my despair and brought healing for my pain. Pouring out my deep sadness to my God brought us closer. On the side of the road, He slowly and steadily calmed my anxious soul and began to speak the words I needed to hear.

God is not afraid when we lay it all out with Him. He does not hold it against us when we disagree strongly and let Him know it. In fact, He welcomes it. We are invited to lay all our burdens on Him. He will not collapse under the load, or storm off with His hands over his ears. David was a man after God's own heart, yet He asked God directly why He had abandoned Him. David knew that hiding his rage would not promote intimacy with God, but only distance. The wife that asks her pouting husband what is wrong and receives a curt "nothing" knows her husband's restraint is not respect, but isolation. We do the same in our relationship with God when we avoid crying out to Him and retreat to our rooms, slamming the door behind us. There is, of course, an important difference between complaining and lamenting to God that I will discuss in the final chapter. For now, ask yourself if you are avoiding your relationship with God by refusing to lament the pain you have experienced in your dating life.

Risk

Risk is an indispensable part of any relationship. To walk in faith requires you to step out into the unknown without knowing the outcome. God will frequently send us on paths with only enough light to show us the next step. The same is true in dating relationships. Your relationship with someone special will be rather bland if it fails to call anything out of you that is unexpected. Meeting strangers, initiating conversation, dialing a phone number, opening yourself to intimacy, having the courage to speak the truth, and finding the strength to walk down the aisle, or walk away – all of it requires risk. If a relationship is too easy, too predictable, then it is probably built on dishonesty. The danger for all singles is to develop the fear of taking risks.

My friend, Luke, has shown me the importance of taking risks in the realm of relationships. His desire for marriage was thwarted for many years. Relationships came and went, but he could never find the special one with whom to exchange rings. Last fall he was set up on a series of blind dates, but each evening grew more and more frustrating. I won't bore you with the details, but one of them inspired a screenplay for a horror film that became a box office smash. I can remember the dejection and despair on Luke's face when one set-up after another led to a dead end. Though tempted to bury himself in his work or hobbies, he did not let the disappointment get the best of him. I was amazed when he told me two weeks later that he had another blind date. How much more of this would he take? Nevertheless, he went out that weekend with the willingness to risk again. You know what happened even before I tell you - his blind date in the fall became his wedding the following summer. Ask him now if he regrets taking that last risk.

Listening

I have found no clearer correlation between my relationship with God and my relationship with women than in the need to listen. When I have sat before the throne to listen to my Father's voice, I have been counseled to step forward or to step away in my dating relationships. When I heeded His voice I was thankful weeks later. When I was too busy to listen or followed my own script, I was left with regret as a companion. As our desire to be married intensifies we become more and more prone to rush ahead, manipulate circumstances, and force matches that were conceived in our demands, rather than in heaven.

Perhaps there is no better example of the need to listen to God in our dating than when the time comes to let go of a relationship. How many of us can share a story when we hung on too long, knowing the relationship was unhealthy and had no future? For too many singles when the going gets tough in a relationship, the tough get stubborn. Despite counsel to move on, we are too afraid to be alone. That is just what my friend Ethan did recently. He was in love with a girl who did not feel the same way about him. He did what he could to make the relationship work, but realized they were going in circles. He took the strong road of ending the relationship and moving on, refusing to hold on to a goat rope. The best part is he listened to God and his friends to help him make the right decision. His heart is sad, and he struggles with loneliness, but he knows he is on the right path.

Openness

Openness is also an important characteristic of our relationship with God and the opposite sex. An open heart is the only type of heart that can experience true romance and intimacy. We have all heard story after story of a friend saying they could never, ever, be with someone, and then two years later they are standing at the altar. I take the course of wisdom when I admit that I do not know what the future could bring, who I might date, and what might bring us together. In fact, as I reflect on my past, God has led me on the path I least anticipated in my relationships. I have enjoyed relationships that I had verbally predicted months before would never happen.

Chapter Six – Dating

God first brought me to a point of openness, before blessing me with someone special.

My friend, Shelly, had been frustrated for so long in her desire for a husband that she finally gave up hope. She planned on joining the F.B.I. as a field agent because she heard the work schedule would consume her life leaving precious little time to even think about romance. She submitted her application, was accepted by the Bureau, and was about to start her basic training as a skilled agent and a dead romancer. But alas Shelly's heart was not as closed as she thought. Jesus intervened. She went on a ski trip with some friends, met Jim, took a snowmobile ride with him, and last week I received their wedding invitation in the mail. Shelly opened her heart to romance and God moved in. But it works the other way as well. Show me a heart that is closing itself to romance and I will show you a heart that is closing itself to God.

Generosity

Finally, the same generosity that needs to characterize our relationship with God needs to show up in our dating. Time, words, thoughts, emotions, deeds – these are all gifts that we give and receive in our relationship with our Father. It is important that the same is reflected with our significant other, and not just on Valentine's Day. Some of us struggle to put our feelings into words, and tragically we deny our lover a gift they earnestly desire. Others are afraid to feel wanted because it is a far cry from what we have experienced in the past. We forget that receiving is an inevitable part of generosity. Still others feel uncomfortable when someone wants to do something special for them. They feel they have to pay off the debt and balance the scales. Scripture frequently reminds us to be generous with God, not just with our money but with our whole hearts. The more generous we are with Him, the more generous we become with our sweethearts.

As for the relationship between our love for God and our love for another, much more could be said than what I have suggested here. Consider the importance of understanding, discovering, experimenting, and submission in both of these relationships. It is amazing how much our love for another needs to grow out of our love for God. Anyone who does not admit that love is a mystery never tasted the real thing – with the divine or the human.

A SACRED PURPOSE

I have always held a deep affection for the love stories of the Bible. The stories of Jacob's tireless pursuit of Rachel, Ruth's seduction of Boaz, and even the romantic escapades of Samson have always kept my attention and rekindled my own desire for a romantic encounter. My favorite tale of romance from the Bible, however, is the story of Isaac and Rebekah.

Many parts of this story grow on me every time I read it in Genesis 24. I am awed at Abraham's concern for his son's marriage and his assurance to his servant that God will send his angel ahead of him to help find the right woman. I am amused at the test Abraham's servant contrives to find a wife for Isaac. The description of Rebekah in Genesis 24:16 quickly grabs my attention. She sounds like quite a catch. Her extra efforts to draw water for the servant's camels, and the enthusiasm of her family over God's providence, reaches a climax with the words, "This is from the Lord." (NIV) Rebekah's willingness to leave her home and take the risk to which God was calling her is extraordinary. The beauty of the story is completed when Isaac

Chapter Six – Dating

comes out of the field to see his beautiful bride approaching in the distance. Rebekah descends from her camel, covers her face with a veil, and meets her groom at his tent. Isaac and Rebekah are married, they fall deeply in love, and these two become one, secure in the fact that God Himself had brought them together.

Although I have read this story many times, I recently read it more carefully and caught something that bothers me. As Abraham's servant is about to begin his search for Isaac's wife, he offers a prayer to God that is really unnerving. It doesn't seem to fit. His opening words are, "O Lord, God of my master. Give me success and show kindness to my master, Abraham. Help me to accomplish the purpose of my journey." (Gen. 24:12) What? Show kindness to Abraham? Are you kidding me? Isaac is the one who is going to have to live with this woman. Shouldn't we pray God shows kindness to Isaac? Isn't Isaac's marital happiness the purpose of the servant's journey?

Apparently I missed something. Isaac's dating profile doesn't even get mentioned in this chapter. There is no discussion of Rebekah's compatibility points, Isaac's love languages, or either one's restaurant preferences. The servant seems more concerned with pleasing Abraham than he does Isaac or Rebekah. Why is there greater urgency in this story over God's plan for Abraham than the bride and groom?

I believe God was up to a whole lot more in this chapter than just making sure Isaac had a bachelor party. As always, God had a much grander plan in mind. Even here in the story of Isaac and Rebekah's romance, God was concerned with expanding His kingdom. He was focused on fulfilling His promises to Abraham and enlarging His people. The relationship between Isaac and Rebekah was the backdrop for moving God's plan of redemption forward. No less significant was the fact that the Son of God would be born out of Isaac and Rebekah's descendants. None of this means God did not care about this young couple's marital happiness. Rather, God was accomplishing much, much more than just a wedding. Another chapter was being written in the story of redemption.

Dating is a sacred activity. It is sacred because God is involved and working out a much larger plan in two people's lives than simply a wedding. He always keeps the big picture in mind and loves to multi-task redemption within a single event. Instead of just praying for a lifetime partner, I believe singles should ask God to advance a plan of eternal significance through their romances. We need to ask God the bigger questions as to what He wants to accomplish in our dating. How does He want to use your dating relationships to transform the lives of many people and not just your own? How does God want to use you to bring about special changes in your special someone? What aspects of *your* life does the Lord want to transform through your partner? Praying about the lifetime impact you and a possible spouse could have demonstrates great foresight. How would marrying someone empower the two of you to bring redemption to your workplace, church, or community? No doubt God also has big plans for the children you may have in the future. Dating and marrying the right person suddenly becomes much more significant.

These may seem like weightier and bigger questions than your dating life requires. But I think a trivial attitude about dating leads not only to heartache, but also to a very small vision. God is sovereign over all aspects of His creation – including our candlelit dinners on a Friday night. Consider how exciting it would be to know that God was accomplishing far more in your dating than simply finding you a mate. It thrills me to think that my love life is part of the epic tale God is writing about His redemption and restoration of the universe. Remembering the larger story will allow me to say on my wedding day, like Isaac and Rebekah, "This is from the Lord."

YOU KNOW WHEN YOU KNOW

My grandmother is a very skilled woman. She makes the best chocolate chip cookies in the world, takes care of her own lake house, and is a sharp-shooter with a bee bee gun. She can do almost anything she sets her mind on. Although I do not care for her banana cream pies or knitted sweaters, I do think she is on track with her philosophy of dating. Often she asks me if I have found Miss Right yet. When I reply that I have not she smiles and says, "Well, it's okay. When you do meet her you'll know. You just know when you know."

Maybe she should be writing this book. I agree with her. How much heartache and pain could be avoided in marriages if people just followed that advice. How many separations and divorces would never have occurred if people lived from the inside out rather than the outside in? How many more singles could be free to live, fall in love, and say yes to marriage if they listened to their hearts.

If you are planning to marry someone because you are afraid time is running out, then I beg you to stop and listen. If you are mailing wedding invitations with someone you *think* you could live with, then please get out now. If you are about to walk the aisle with someone who has always been just a good friend and just might make a great mate, then run very quickly the other way. In fact, if you are scheduling your premarital counseling sessions because you are tired of being lonely, then you might as well schedule your marriage crisis counseling sessions as well.

One of the greatest tragedies for singles is to say "I do" when you are really thinking "I'm not sure." Save you and your unwitting victim a lot of pain and be honest about your feelings. What a pity to throw away the adventure of singleness and enter a marriage that your heart is not truly in.

There is a better way - it is the way of walking intimately with Jesus and allowing Him to bring the true desire of your heart to the surface. It is the way of listening to what you want and having the courage to wait on Him for that special someone. It is the way of trusting Him to bring you your spouse. How will you know when He has done so? Listen to Him, listen to your heart. You just know - you just know when you know.

CHAPTER SEVEN

SEX

The beauty of life, is that you don't have to be modernly beautiful to live it.

— C.S. Lewis

One night as I was sleeping, my heart awakened in a dream. I heard the voice of my lover. He was knocking at my bedroom door. 'Open to me, my darling, my treasure, my lovely dove,' he said, 'for I have been out in the night. My head is soaked with dew, my hair with the wetness of the night.' But I said, 'I have taken off my robe. Should I get dressed again? I have washed my feet. Should I get them soiled?' My lover tried to unlatch the door, and my heart thrilled within me. I jumped up to open it. My hands dripped with perfume, my fingers with lovely myrrh, as I pulled back the bolt. I opened to my lover, but he was gone. I yearned for even his voice! I searched for him, but I couldn't find him anywhere. I called to him, but there was no reply.

— (Song of Songs 5:2-6)

The Single Journey

Two years ago on a Friday afternoon a female coworker approached me with a rather unexpected proposition. It was an offer I did not see coming, but my decision that day changed my life. We had worked together for three years and had become good friends. She was young, blonde, and a lot of fun. She was also married. Her husband would be out of town for the weekend thus altering their plans and presenting me with a unique opportunity. I only briefly pondered her offer and then accepted. My life has not been the same since that day.

I accepted her gift of two tickets to that weekend's stock car race at Daytona International Speedway - since her husband had been called out of town, she wanted to give away the tickets. I went with a friend to the race the next day. From the first lap to the last I was converted. Henceforth, I have become a racing fan.

I had always thought NASCAR races would be rather boring. What could be interesting about cars going around and around in a circle? But when, for the first time, I stood in the stands as forty-three cars came rushing around turn two at 190 mph, I knew I had been missing out on something great! Just the roar of so many cars whizzing by me was an adrenaline rush. The smell of oil, spilled fuel, and hot engines filled the air. Pit crews scrambled around the cars to change tires, refuel, and make adjustments - all under fourteen seconds. Fans cheered for their favorite driver, hoping and praying he would be the first to cross the finish line. And of course the day would just not be complete if we did not see five, no eight, no, even better, ten cars spin out of control and pile into each other. It is just all part of the sport. *(I'm sure you are wondering what all this talk about cars has to do with sex, but just bare with me for a moment. I'm a guy; I have trouble separating the two.)*

Chapter Seven - Sex

The longer I am a NASCAR fan the more interested I become in the science of racing. Yes, there is a science to it. Race teams will do whatever it takes to shave one-hundredth of a second off their lap times. Aerodynamic sheet metal, the right tires, finding the right groove, a skilled driver – all are important in order to be fastest on the track. Most importantly, however, is a racecar's handling. If a driver cannot control the handling of his car it does not matter how fast he is because he will not be able to turn when necessary. If a car is not balanced as it travels around the track then the driver will face one of two problems: oversteering or understeering.

A race car is oversteering or "loose" when it overreacts to a turn of the steering wheel. Driving smoothly around the corner is difficult because the back end of the car begins to slide up the track and take the front end with it. The driver quickly looses control of the car and backs into the wall as the wheels *over-respond* to his commands. Ultimately, the driver has no power over the car because the handling is too independent and unrestrained.

A race car is understeering or "tight" when it reacts too little to a turn of the steering wheel. The car *under-responds* to the driver's commands, making it impossible to round the corner. Instead, the race car will head straight for the wall. A pricey car is wrecked, not because the wheels had too much freedom, but because they had too little.

What does this lesson in a race car's handling have to do with sex? It is a convenient metaphor to understand the two extremes singles lean towards with their sexuality. What do singles do without a spouse with whom to enjoy healthy, balanced, sexual intimacy? They either oversteer or understeer. Their sexuality and their desire for sexual intercourse, and the two are not the same, becomes wild and erratic or denied and deadened. Neither one, nor the other, is what God desires for our sexuality as neither leaves us in control of our bodies. Both are slavery and keep us from the freedom in which we are invited to live.

These two ways of handling our sexuality reveal an improper and limited perspective. Thankfully, the Bible gives us a much more balanced and liberated view which I will try to outline in the second half of this chapter. First, allow me to expand on the two damaging extremes that singles, and for that matter all humans, tend to lean towards with their sexuality. And by the way, I still feel no guilt about accepting that married woman's offer, but please do not quote that line out of context.

OVERSTEERING

It can be a pretty scary experience to drive 200 mph and have the car turn too much. You can turn the steering wheel a little, but the wheels over-respond and you spin out of control. Singles that do not have their sexuality under control can be just like a spinning race car. For the moment it all seems exciting and dramatic, but the consequences can be devastating.

Out of control is a good way to describe many singles and sex. Virginity used to be considered a gift to give to one's life partner. Now it is treated like the chicken pox. Get it over with so you don't have to worry about it anymore. As a result, if you make it into your twenties or thirties and you are still a single virgin, you qualify for the endangered species list. The world celebrates those who have the most sexual partners, and if one waits until the fourth date to have sex then there must be a problem. Sadly, many Christian singles are not far behind the world. Despite the prohibitions of Scripture, plenty of believers end up going all the way before marriage.

It does not matter if you read the Bible upside down, on your head, or hanging from the ceiling, God's Word forbids sex outside of marriage. In Numbers 25, God brought judgment on the Israelites for their lack of restraint. Paul told the Corinthians that each man should enjoy his own wife and each wife should enjoy her own husband for the sake of purity (I Cor. 7). Paul told Timothy, who was young and probably single, to treat the younger women with the same purity as he would his own sister (I Tim. 5:2). Jesus, Himself, elevated the sanctity of marriage and sex to unprecedented heights by emphasizing the union of two hearts becoming one flesh brought together by God (Matt. 19:6).

Ironically, singles that indulge their desire for sex prematurely do not have an open mind about sex, but rather a limited mind. When we settle for extramarital sex we are missing out on the real thing. We miss out on the union of two bodies brought even closer together by a lifetime commitment, for better or for worse. Sex that leaves us wondering when our partner might up and leave is not sexual intimacy; it is just using another body to reach orgasm. C.S. Lewis put it this way:

> *We are half-hearted creatures, fooling about with drink and sex and ambition when infinite joy is offered us, like an ignorant child who wants to go on making mud pies in a slum because he cannot imagine what is meant by the offer of a holiday at the sea. We are far too easily pleased.*
> — (from *The Weight of Glory*)

Jumping out of a second story window is a lot more exhilarating than sitting in a chair, but eventually you will feel the consequences. Promiscuous sex is pretty much the same thing. It results in less freedom rather than greater freedom. It is unrestrained sexuality. It is a lack of control. It is oversteering.

Pornography also sends sexuality spinning out of control. If the availability of magazines, strip bars, and peep shows was not enough, we are now barraged by obscene cable television and email. It used to take some measure of courage to get access to pornography. At least you had to show a cashier what you were buying. Now you do not have to seek out pornography; it seeks you.

I grieve over the number of souls, mostly men, that have been eaten alive by the cancer of pornography. I have yet to talk to a male who struggles with pornography and at the same time feels strong and assured in his masculinity. That is, of course, the irony of the images. Pornography makes us men feel like men, but yet requires nothing manly of us. We lie to ourselves when we think we are just trying to catch a glimpse of naked body parts. We linger too long in a magazine, or in front of a computer screen, because we are looking for life, approval, and love. Pope John Paul was right when he said the problem with pornography is not that it shows too much of a woman, but rather too little. We only see her body and not her heart. We are missing out on what we really want. Viewing a centerfold requires a lot less risk than pursuing the heart of a real woman. No guy ever gets turned down or ignored by a picture. Only real female flesh and blood can do that, yet it is also the only place where we can find the true and deep intimacy we really want.

Unfortunately there are a lot of lies being pedaled today about pornography. We are told that it is the right of an adult, a simple pleasure, and spice for the marriage bed. This could not be more false! The truth is pornography is destructive to our very biology. Just as the consumption of too much salt eventually leaves the best of meals tasting bland, so too if we condition our sexual response to a computer screen, when it comes time to enjoy sexual intimacy with our spouse we may find things to be pretty bland. Our taste buds were made for multiple flavors, but our sexuality was not made for multiple partners.

Extramarital sex and pornography are not the only ways singles allow their sexuality to spin out of control. Lust, plain and simple, is an uncontrolled desire for something that is not ours. Undressing and using another's body to satisfy our minds is not passion and romance, it is manipulation and degradation. Compulsive masturbation is not liberating, but rather enslaving. Relationships obsessed with the physical do not mean two people are made for each other, rather that they have little self-control. I know singles who use their bodies like flypaper to catch the unsuspecting. They say it is all part of the game. I say I do not want to play a game. I want a lifetime of romance.

God has given us an incredible gift in our desire for sex. It is charged with energy and exhilaration, like a speeding race car headed into turn three. All the more reason to exercise self-control. What a scary thing when our sexuality is out of bounds and unmanageable. As much as we turn the wheel the car is all over the place and we are out of the groove. The steering is too loose. We are spinning out of control praying we do not hit something; like a cement wall, which is exactly where you are headed if your car is too tight. No matter how hard you turn the wheel it will not respond. There is no control. There is no freedom. This is understeering. No way to turn. No where to go, and here comes the wall.

UNDERSTEERING

A strange notion has crept into the thinking of many Christian singles – the notion that sexuality is synonymous with lust and immorality. Somehow many have arrived at the conclusion that our bodies do not matter, attention to appearance is superficial, and attraction and flirting is always dishonest. Regardless of how we hold ourselves on the outside, people are supposed to look only at our insides. After all, does not God only look at the inside and ignore the outside?

I think a false distinction is being made here. Of course God is more concerned with our hearts than our hairstyles, but when we have been changed on the inside others should be able to see a difference on the outside. It has been said that the eye is the window to the soul. I know there is something wrong in a heart when I see a vacant or empty look in someone's eyes. Yet I see a sparkle in the eyes of those whose hearts are alive. The same is true of our sexuality. If we are alive and free on the inside, that redemption will carry over to our sexuality. Paula Rinehart calls it a window to the heart. What we do with our sexuality reflects what we have done with our hearts.

I am concerned about the hearts of many singles. They have bought the lie that godliness deadens sexuality. Sanctification does not equal frumpiness. When did brown and gray become Christianity's official colors? If our life in Christ is supposed to be contagious and inviting, then why do so many believers live the life of a wallflower? I worry about a guy who is too self-conscious to take his shirt off at the beach. A pretty girl who hides her beauty beneath sweat pants and pulled back hair is saying more about her heart than her appearance.

Body shame was one of the first indicators Adam and Eve knew something was wrong after the Fall. Suddenly their glorious bodies seemed embarrassing. Shameful. Dirty. They ran and hid as fast as they could. Not until the Lord covered them with animal skins did they begin to feel a measure of confidence again. And confidence is exactly what the body of Christ should feel. We are the living, breathing, walking, talking body of Jesus on the earth today. Even more, we are the temple of God wherein the very Spirit of God dwells. This is what a redeemed sexuality proclaims. This is the only standard of body image that matters. Why would we compare ourselves to anyone else?

But this kind of assurance is rare. Often Christians associate being attractive with being worldly and materialistic. What we often settle for is a muted sexuality. We give the same attention to the temple of God that we give to items stored in the attic. We become so out of touch with our bodies and desires that we think any physical contact or expression will lead to lust and sex. I get the same feeling around such singles that I do when I need to adjust the brightness level on my TV.

I realize in making these remarks that I run the risk of being written off as vane and pretentious. Perhaps for my female readers this all sounds sexist and easier said than done. (*I was recently informed that a full length mirror is a woman's greatest enemy.*) But what I am getting at is that wounds from our past, or a frustrated desire for sex when we do not have a spouse, can provoke some of us to push our sexuality underground. Christians, more than anyone else, have the only reason to rejoice in our sexuality. All of our shame has been taken away. We can celebrate one of the greatest gifts God has given us. Anything less is fear. Hiding. Control. Understeering.

PIT STOP

The Apostle Paul faced an interesting dilemma in the Corinthian church. Apparently a group of false teachers were spreading the lie that since Christians receive new bodies at the resurrection, then our current bodies do not matter in this life. In fact, they claimed that since our bodies have no value, it does not matter what we do with them – including visiting the local temples and having sex with its many prostitutes.

I think Paul rolled up his sleeves and cracked his knuckles before he took on these heretics. When he takes up his pen to rebuke them in I Corinthians 6, he pulls no punches and drives them into the ground with some of his best theology. Listen to his words:

> ... *our bodies were not made for sexual immorality. They were made for the Lord, and the Lord cares about our bodies. And God will raise our bodies from the dead by his marvelous power, just as he raised our Lord from the dead. Don't you realize that your bodies are actually parts of Christ? Should a man take his body, which belongs to Christ, and join it to a prostitute? Never!... Or don't you know that your body is the temple of the Holy Spirit, who lives in you and was given to you by God? You do not belong to yourself, for God bought you with a high price. So you must honor God with your body.*
>
> - (I Cor. 6:13a-15, 19-20)

The false teachers must have had a hard time refuting Paul's arguments in these words. He asked them how they could take something so glorious as our bodies and give them over to a prostitute. Did they not understand that the Spirit of God dwells in our bodies? Did they not know that Christ cares so much about our bodies that He paid the ultimate price for them? Jesus died to redeem our bodies; so we must treat them with the same honor God gives them.

Paul was livid that the Corinthians were accepting a lie about the body to justify sexual immorality. Recklessness. Oversteering. I doubt he would be any happier today to know the same argument is being used to justify the other extreme. Sexual deadness. Blandness. Understeering.

It is a crippling error to think that our sexuality is only about what happens between the sheets with another body. Our sexuality is so much more a part of us than that; it is so much grander than that. Our sexuality is a fundamental part of who we are. It is as foundational and encompassing to our identity as our personality, emotions, desires, and distastes. We are walking, talking, breathing, sexual beings, not just when we are having sex or talking about sex, but all day, every day, we are sexually expressing ourselves. The way we sit, stand, walk, and talk, the way we read, drive, eat, and sleep, the way we listen, yawn, dress, ask for directions, or sign our name – all of this is sexual expression. Hollywood is wrong. Everyone is sexy. It is just that some know it and some do not.

Certainly the Bible places a greater value on the inside rather than the outside, but you will search its pages in vain to find a place where it says the outside is of no importance. It does not condone sexual immorality and neither does it endorse a muted sexuality. In fact the Scriptures praise the glory of each gender. Psalm 45 was written as a wedding song, but it is a joyful celebration of each gender and the appeal each has for the other.

The great blessing of the gospel is that regardless of where we have been with our sexuality in the past, things can be different in the future. Irrespective of what we have done in the past, genuine change is not only a possibility, but it is God's deep desire for us. A life that is born again by Jesus Christ includes a redeemed sexuality. Neither oversteering nor understeering is beyond His ability to repair. Jesus is the ultimate mechanic, able to repair or replace any of our broken parts; we just need to make a pit stop.

Race cars that handle well and are not oversteering or understeering are said to be balanced. The wheels respond smoothly to the turn of the wheel and it feels like you are going for a Sunday drive. You can put the car exactly where you want it and it responds perfectly. In the groove is exactly where you want to be. The groove is the lane around the race track that is the best path for speed and stability. This is the place where you will be the smoothest, the fastest, and most successful. What does redeemed sexuality look like when it is in the groove?

IN THE GROOVE

Our enemy is a crook. He is not only the father of lies, but also a master thief. He steals the good gifts of God, adds his own evil twist, and then sells them as his own. Just think what the Evil One has done with good things like music, wine, work, marriage, and sex. One of his favorite things to steal are words. One of the crucial words he has stolen from the truth is seduction.

The word seduction has become full of all kinds of sexual connotations. It is hard to imagine a seductive scene in a movie that would not involve two people spending the night together. But allow me to suggest that Christians need to take this word back from the world's corruption. There is a better meaning to this word that does not require a bedroom. In fact, it is a word that only the reborn can claim as their own.

The original meaning of the word seduce is "to take aside." Perhaps the original meaning was to take someone aside into the bedroom, but I do not think it requires that. When we live the life for which we were originally created, we will be taking people aside all the time. Taking them out of their element. Taking them off guard. Taking them away from the unexpected. There will be something so captivating, so contagious, and so attractive about us that others will be taken aside – they will be seduced.

I am not talking about manipulation here; this is not about tight clothing or immodest necklines. This is about living out our identities in Christ. We have been given new hearts, new desires, and new lives. Should not that inner reality be evidenced on the outside? Nothing can separate us from God's love. No one else has as much reason to love, risk, hope, and embrace life as we do. The world pursues ultimate makeovers to reconstruct the outside, but what really needs reconstruction is the inside. When we truly live from our identity in Christ, we exhibit the ultimate sex appeal. Followers of Jesus become the most seductive singles around.

It may sound "spiritual" to say that outward beauty does not matter, looks are irrelevant, and only a person's inner beauty is important, but I confess such an admission would be dishonest. The truth is, attraction is important to me. The Bible places value on it as well. Scripture points out that Absalom was the best looking guy in Israel. In fact, in II Samuel 14:25, it says he had the perfect body. In Genesis 29:17, Rachel is described as a very attractive woman. Of course, I do not need to remind you of the entire book of Song of Songs.

A heart alive on the inside will demonstrate genuine seduction on the outside in three ways: countenance, cosmetics, and characteristics. I am sure my male readers are really getting worried about me now, so let me quickly explain.

Your countenance is what your face displays. You begin communicating with your face well before you open your mouth. What do you see when you look in the mirror? Joy? Sadness? Despair? Acceptance? These are all traits that others can read from our countenance whether we want them to or not. The Bible says the wages of sin is death (Rom. 6:23). Do not be deceived. Sin is always destructive to our hearts and a lifetime of sin will show itself on our countenance (Prov. 15:13). I am sure you have met people who have done a lot of hard living; you can see it in their eyes.

But the same is true for those who have had the light turned on inside. The godly men and women I know in their elder years still have a winsome smile on their face. Sure they have wrinkles, gray hair, and bald spots, but their countenance also reflects peace and assurance. It is a look that says they have walked a thousand miles, but have not been alone. The Son of God was with them the whole way. There is something deeply attractive about a single guy or girl with a bright countenance. It is not something you practice in front of the mirror, rather it spills over from an inside washed clean with forgiveness.

Cosmetics also need to be part of your seductive self. This is not all about make-up, guys, so relax. It is about how we decorate the temple of the body wherein God's Spirit dwells. The Temple in the Old Testament was ornamented with the finest materials to highlight its significance as a meeting place between God and His people. How much more can we celebrate our bodies because Christ dwells inside? The world makes much of shopping, clothes, and jewelry as if our significance could be found in these things. Unlike the world Christians really do have a reason to appreciate our bodies. We should also have the best tans. We do not have to earn God's approval so that leaves more time to go to the beach.

The actress, Elisabeth Rohm, has said, "The clothes you wear reflect the things that are hidden deep inside of you. They're a statement about something close to your world. Fashion is a way of turning yourself inside out." She is right. What we wear says something about our heart. Body posture, clothes, hair, eye contact – all of this says more about our self-perceptions than what was on sale last week. Why not decorate our temples like they are the dwelling place of God? Now we are talking about genuine attraction and seduction.

I have already mentioned my love for the ocean and the beach. I cannot get enough of the sand, the sun, and the waves. It is my paradise. Alright, so maybe a day at the beach would not be complete for me if I did not watch a few bikinis pass by So sue me - I'm a guy. However, what I find interesting is that out of all the lovely ladies I have seen on the beach I only remember one of them. She was medium height with long, brown hair. She stood at the shore and let the water run through her toes. She wore a red bikini. She was beautiful in every way. She was also nine months pregnant. I think the reason I remember her was because she was not hiding her loveliness despite a very large belly. She was thumbing her nose at the world's standard as to what sexuality needs to look like and who gets to wear a bikini. She was femininity at its best. What great courage! What great freedom!

Attention to appearance is not the same as vanity. Vanity is finding your identity in your appearance. Paul did not condemn improving your looks, as is commonly thought. Paul warned the women in Timothy's church against focusing on hair braiding and wearing expensive jewelry because their decadent appearance was inappropriate during worship (I Tim. 2:8-10). Timothy's city, Ephesus, was known for its temple prostitution and rampant immorality. Paul forbade women from coming to church who were dressed for the brothel.

Finally, rejoice in your unique characteristics as expressions of your seductive self. Actress Charlotte Rampling has said, "Beauty is not necessarily beautiful features. It's about understanding one's style and having the attitude to carry off that style." How can you express your individuality and express who you are on the outside? If you are wondering how you can change to look like your favorite celebrity, you are asking the wrong question. Rather, what can you do on the outside that expresses who you are on the inside?

I am expressing who I am when I wear my favorite pair of jeans, a sleeveless shirt, my puca shell necklace, and a dash of cologne. On a good day, when I have the courage, I might even wear my cowboy hat to the beach. Believe it or not, it is not about getting attention. It is just what I like. It is me.

Our sexuality runs a lot deeper in our souls than just a desire for intercourse. It is part of our identity, and what we do with it is very important. If our sexuality is redeemed and alive, then I believe it will take people aside; they will find it seducing. Our countenance, cosmetics, and characteristics are simply ways we can express on the outside who we truly are on the inside. This is the kind of sexuality God smiles upon. It is contagious, inviting, glorious. It is driving around the track in control and in the groove. There is no better place to be. Well, ...maybe one place.

YELLOW FLAG

When there is a crash or multiple car wreck in a NASCAR race the flag man waves a yellow flag. All the other race cars slow down while safety crews rescue trapped drivers, put out fires, and tow away damaged cars. The race is under caution. Even if you were not involved in the wreck, you must drive at a crawling speed and not pass the other cars. Several hundred horsepower under the hood are begging you to put the accelerator to the floor, but it is not the time. You have to wait for the green flag before you can go back to racing. You have to wait.

If we intend to honor God with our desire for genuine sexual intimacy, it will take patient waiting. We know we have plenty of horsepower under the hood, plenty of desire for sexual union, but God does not wave the green flag until wedding vows are exchanged.

As I have said above I do not think this means Christian singles need to live with a dead sexuality. It is unwise to kill what is a fundamental part of who we are. But it does mean our desire for intercourse may not be fulfilled for some time. This can be quite a challenge in a sex obsessed culture. What do we do with the longings of the flesh as we wait for a honeymoon?

I think one of the best steps we can take is to acknowledge the desire as natural and good. It is alright to admit that our bodies are ready to become one flesh with another. This is something we can celebrate. Our desire for sex is one of God's greatest gifts. It should be appreciated. This is not the same as lust, which is idolatry. It is gratitude to God for giving us something so mysterious and special as our desire to be one with a lover.

Self-control must, however, be the course we chart on the single journey. This is not a selfish and stifling type of control. This is the liberating ownership of the self that is a fruit of the Spirit (Gal. 5:23). The desire for sex is a drive, not a need. If we believe the drive has more power than it really does, we will allow it to master us. But when our heart is in order, it is amazing how quickly this desire falls into its place as well, becoming part of us rather than the master of us.

I believe a much greater fuss has been made over masturbation than is necessary. Self-pleasuring is a personal decision to be made by you on your single journey. It is an entirely appropriate and healthy means of releasing the physical craving for sex. A whole battery of Bible verses have been mustered to condemn the practice as ungodly and destructive. But Scripture is silent on the subject of masturbation. Self-pleasuring is a decision that needs to be made by you in the context of your faith. Masturbation has a lot more to do with the motives of your heart, than the arbitrary rules of others.

One of the best ways we can avoid being overwhelmed by our physical desire is by pursuing genuine connection with others. Isolating ourselves at home when there are friends to be made and dates to be enjoyed only makes our desire for physical intimacy fester. The desire to touch and be touched can be redirected simply by pursuing a connection at the level of the heart with others. Intimacy of the heart is often more powerful and more enduring than the intimacy of touch.

Yet, when it all comes right down to it, our desire for sex will not be truly satisfied until we become one flesh with our spouse, as God originally intended. If we find ourselves yearning for Song of Songs intimacy in the meantime, then our hearts are in the right place. We are left with something good. We are left with hope - hope that says our hearts and desires are still alive and well, but we are patiently, eagerly awaiting the right moment. The moment after rings are exchanged, vows are made, and the two of you are pronounced as husband and wife. Then the guests are dismissed, the two of you are alone, the door is closed, and the green flag waves. The engine roars. The tires spin. You have left everyone else in the dust. At last. Victory. Sweet victory.

The Single Journey

CHAPTER EIGHT

HOPE

They who turn back now know only the ordeal, but they who persevere remember the adventure.
              - Milo L. Arnold

The resurrection life you received from God is not a timid, grave-tending life. It's adventurously expectant, greeting God with a childlike 'What's next, Papa?' God's Spirit touches our spirits and confirms who we really are. We know who he is, and we know who we are: Father and children. And we know we are going to get what's coming to us — an unbelievable inheritance! We go through exactly what Christ goes through. If we go through the hard times with him, then we're certainly going to go through the good times with him.
              - (Rom. 8:15-17; *The Message*)

Heaven seems very far away. At times I have tried to imagine what it will be like to live in a perfect paradise with no sadness, disease, or pain. I close my eyes and try to picture a world with no broken friendships, no unfulfilled dreams, and no boring blind dates. I confess though I am not really successful. Apparently, my faith is weaker than I thought. Maybe my imagination is out of shape. It just seems too hard to keep the mindset that someday the address of God's children will change from dusty roads of sadness to streets paved with gold.

In the meantime, as I wait for the new heavens and new earth, I turn on the radio. I find my favorite songs and turn them up real loud. As we wait for heaven God has given us a few things in this life to whet our appetite for the sweet by and by. The rest that comes with a Sunday afternoon nap, the cool, clean air after the rain, a glass of wine, a sunset that takes your breath away, a gentle kiss... all of these are God's good gifts, appetizers of heaven, to remind His children that someday things will be a whole lot better. All the heartache and disappointment will be forgotten and life will be as it was meant to be.

Music is one of these appetizers. It is one of God's greatest gifts. Music has a unique power to take us out of our circumstances and transport us to a different place. How is it that music can reach so deep into our hearts, and the stories of our lives, and unexpectedly take us back to painful memories or happier times? Why do I get so charged up when I hear "Welcome to the Jungle" at a hockey game? How come I can sing "How Great Thou Art" at a friend's funeral and yet still mean it? There is nothing quite like a song or a few notes to penetrate our hearts and wake us up inside, whether we want to or not.

When loneliness threatens to strangle me, and I can't stand to be single anymore, God uses music to comfort me, awaken me, calm me, and inspire me. Although the Almighty seems to be pretty eclectic in His musical tastes, if you are going to buy me a CD, make mine country. I have developed something of an addiction to the sound of steel guitars, fiddles, mandolins, and twangy voices. Something in its stories, familiar lyrics, and good times attitude captures me and invites me to sing along. Maybe all the songs about home subtlety remind me that a better residence awaits me above.

Many times God has caught me off guard with the lyrics of a song. Recently, a song sung by Sara Evans got my attention; it just seemed to capture the longings of a single's heart. The name of the song is "Born to Fly."

> *I've been telling my dreams to the scarecrow*
> *About the places that I'd like to see*
> *I say, 'friend do you think I'll ever get there?'*
> *Oh, but he just stands there smilin' back at me*
> *So I confessed my sins to the preacher*
> *About the love I've been prayin' to find*
> *Is there a brown-eyed boy in my future, yeah*
> *And he says, 'girl, you've got nothin' but time.'*
>
> *But how do you wait for heaven?*
> *And who has that much time?*
> *And how do you keep your feet on the ground*
> *When you know that you were born,*
> *You were born to fly*
>
> *My daddy he is grounded like the oak tree*
> *My momma she is steady as the sun*
> *Oh, you know I love my folks*
> *But I keep starin' down the road*
> *Just lookin' for my one chance to run*
> *Hey, cause I will soar away like a black bird*
> *I will blow in the wind like a seed*

*I will plant my heart in the garden of my dreams
And I will grow up where I wander wild and free*

*Oh, how do you wait for heaven?
And who has that much time?
And how do you keep your feet on the ground
When you know, that you were born?
You were born, yeah, you were born to fly.*

- *(Born to Fly,* Copyright 2000)

I really like those lyrics. They capture how I feel a lot of the time. What do you do when you are single and really want to be married? What do you do when you are not sure you will ever exchange rings? What do you do when you want to soar like the blackbird, but you are still alone? What do you do when your friends are getting married and you are not? What do you do while you wait for heaven? Most of all what do you do when your feet are still on the ground and you know, *you just know,* you were born to fly?

The Apostle Paul said three things remain: faith, hope, and love. We need faith to believe God's grace and the kingdom identity He has given us. We need love in our relationships with our friends, mentors, and lovers. But it is that middle word I often struggle to hold onto. What does it mean to hope when things have always been this way? How do I know whether I am holding onto genuine hope, or just fooling myself that things will be different? People tell me not to give up hope and that my dreams for a spouse will one day come true. But how can they be sure? Just what exactly is hope?

Chapter Eight - Hope

THE PULSE OF DESIRE

I fear that somewhere in all the pages I have written that I might have implied there is a way to eliminate the sadness and loneliness that often accompanies singleness. I do not want anyone to finish reading this book and walk away thinking they now know how to "do" singleness. The truth is the single journey is often filled with sadness, frustration, disappointment, and deep loneliness. These painful emotions are not unique to the single journey, but are the most common during this stretch of our lives. Of course joy comes along the way as well. There is wisdom to be applied, dreams to pursue, and an abundant life to be enjoyed. Yet, as long as our hearts are alive and we open ourselves up to new experiences and relationships, there will be plenty of heartache along the way. The struggles on this leg of the journey cannot be "fixed." God is not waiting for us to figure our way out of the maze. He is calling us to walk across this terrain following His lead. Singleness, like all of life, is as John Eldredge has said - not a problem to be solved, but rather an adventure to be lived.

Hope is our indicator to let us know if we are living that adventure or still trying to fix the problem. Hope is the gauge on the dashboard telling us there is fuel in the tank for the trip ahead. It is the pulse of desire. You know a motionless body is not dead when you can find a pulse. You can tell a single has not let their heart die when they still have hope. Even though our dreams for a spouse have gone unfulfilled, we are still alive with desire, confidently and expectantly waiting for God's best. Only children with a benevolent Father can live with such expectation, and the good news is He never gives His children a stone when they ask Him for bread.

Recently a lot of people have told me I need to get "unsingled." A lot of the advice has sounded fairly spiritual. If I just tell God I do not care about getting married and give up the hunt, then He will be able to give me a spouse. Or if I just pray to be single for the rest of my life then God will break down, snap His fingers, and give me a mate. Somebody recently told me to just marry anybody, and then I will understand my need for God's grace for the rest of my life.

All of that counsel sounds devout and sacrificial. If I went around spouting those lines I would be labeled the most spiritual guy in town. The fundamental problem with all of that counsel, however, is that it puts me at the center of the equation, and assumes that I am in control of events. Even worse, it makes God out to be a puzzle master who is waiting for me to make the right move, knock on the right door, or pray the right prayer. It is my effort to try and solve the "problem" of singleness.

Holding onto hope requires more risk. It includes letting go of our solutions and strategies and asking God to show us His plan. It is admitting our ignorance in our ability to find the love we have always dreamt about. It is far different than pretending we do not care about getting married. Keeping hope means maintaining the desire while enjoying the adventure along the way. Hope keeps us alive even when there is no one special for us anywhere in sight. Singles that say it is too hard to keep hoping and kill the desire for a mate have already lost. They have given up the single journey, turned around, and are traveling the wrong way.

The reason why holding onto hope is not a silly, frivolous pastime is because our hope is not in ourselves - it is in Almighty God. Our hope is based on His good character and solid promises. God's children do not *think* things will work out well; they *know* things will work out well. All things work out well for those who love Him and are called according to His purpose (Rom. 8:28). It may not be what we expect or pursue, but if our story is being written by a gracious Father, then in the end we will be able to look back over the plot and agree with Him that it was good.

Knowing this truth comforts me because it removes any pressure I might put on myself to plot the course ahead or second guess decisions I made yesterday. It is not my job to *solve* the single journey; it is my job to *enjoy Him* on the single journey. I need to follow His lead. He has not forgotten me. He knows each of His children uniquely and loves them specifically. He is always, always working behind the scenes on their behalf. Putting our hope in Him keeps us alive and free.

Hope also makes us more attractive. I am drawn to people who are alive and confidently expectant of the future. I want to be near them hoping that some of it rubs off on me. Those who abandon their desire for lasting love reveal a lot more about their hearts than they realize. Giving up on romance is often surrounded by abandoned dreams, cold friendships, and monotonous schedules; however, singles who are full of hope are more likely to be the ones pursuing and being pursued. Hopeful singles are attractive singles.

A prolonged single journey is the toughest journey I have ever taken. Many times I have wanted to just lay down in the road, find a shortcut, or turn around and go the other way. It is the gift of hope that lifts me up, brushes me off, and helps me take the next step. Hope is my pulse. It tells me my desire for union with another is not dead. I am still alive. I must keep taking steps because the one who gave me my new heart will keep it beating, and promises me I will have His strength and presence for the road ahead.

PERSEVERING

When I was in high school I joined the track team and made my bid to become a world class sprinter. I put a lot into my training, adopted a new diet, and went to the track constantly to improve my lap times. I felt confident about my abilities as our first track meet approached. When the gun sounded for my event, I bolted off the line and kept a steady stride around the first turn. I was in the lead and my school was cheering for me. As I rounded turn two, still in the lead, my friends came to their feet to watch me run.

Yet, as I started to make my way down the backstretch of the quarter-mile track, I noticed I was losing my edge. My heart was racing and my skin was on fire. My side ached from a cramp that grew tighter and tighter. I had started too fast; I had not paced myself. Soon I was passed by one, then two, then three runners. The backstretch seemed much longer than I remembered and I wanted to stop and lay down. I was gasping for breath. Finally, I made it into turn three, but even the slowest runners had passed me. I was at the back of the pack and not sure if I was going to do a header into the asphalt. As I entered the last turn, everyone else had already crossed the finish line. All I could see was a lonely stretch ahead of me, and I refused to walk in front of the grandstand, holding my side, sucking air. I tried to save face by stepping off the track, hoping none of the two thousand people would notice, but of course they did notice, and many of them asked me later why I had given up. I thought it was obvious. I was out of strength, out of breath, and out of pride because I had no perseverance. I had trained for speed, but not distance. I knew how to get a good start and grab the lead, but nobody told me how to keep going.

"Keep going" are two words I have to tell myself often on the single journey. There are plenty of times, after a dead end date or lonely Friday night, that I want to collapse on the track because I am out of breath and out of hope. I suspect I am not alone. The singles scene in any city is full of bored men and resigned women who started the race with a sprint, lost their breath when it got long, and stepped off the track pretending they did not care about the journey in the first place.

I hope the pages of this book have offered you some wisdom to help you keep going on your journey, even when you are out of breath and exhausted. There is no recipe or formula for mastering this journey, but there is plenty of encouragement to help us reach the finish line. When the cramps get painful and my feet get tired, remembering some of the following truths has helped me from losing all hope.

Lamenting helps me to hope when my circumstances are far from encouraging. It is a practice given little attention these days, but was regularly employed by the ancients who put words to the pain of this life. If we are honest we will admit this world is full of pain and hurt. Everyday we interact with people who have short-circuited dreams and believe destructive lies about God, others, and themselves. Everyday your office, classroom, or job site is filled with men and women who shed tears, at least on the inside, because they are mired in debt, their health is failing, their kids hate them, their spouse is cheating, or a beloved friend has passed away.

Grieving is not only cleansing, but healthy for our hearts. I had wanted to be married to a lifetime partner by now. Even more, I believe I was created for such a relationship. But that natural desire remains unfulfilled. As a result I am sad. Why would I not be? Of course my only reason for living is not marriage, but it is still a deep desire of mine. Why would I not pour out that pain to my Father, the ruler of the kingdom? I do grave damage to my heart and my relationship to God when I toss my head back and say, "Never mind. It doesn't matter. I did not want it anyway." The Bible refers to this as a hard heart, a heart that cannot be moved anymore by beauty or pain.

Lamenting lets our hearts breath and stay alive even when our longings have been denied. King David was known as a mighty man of God, but listen to his lament in Psalm 142.

> *I cry out to the Lord;*
> *I plead for the Lord's mercy.*
> *I pour out my complaints before him*
> *and tell him all my troubles.*
> *For I am overwhelmed,*
> *and you alone know the way I should turn.*
> *Wherever I go,*
> *my enemies have set traps for me.*
> *I look for someone to come and help me,*
> *but no one gives me a passing thought!*
> *No one will help me;*
> *no one cares a bit what happens to me.*
> *Then I pray to you, O Lord.*
> *I say, 'You are my place of refuge.*
> *You are all I really want in life.*
> *Hear my cry,*
> *for I am very low.*
> *Rescue me from my persecutors,*
> *for they are too strong for me.*
> *Bring me out of prison*
> *so I can thank you.*

Chapter Eight - Hope

*The godly will crowd around me,
for you treat me kindly.*

Being honest and open with God calms an anxious mind and a troubled heart. Many times I have lamented my loneliness to God and even though He did not immediately change my circumstances, I did feel His touch and His satisfaction. He adjusted my perspective and restored my hope.

Lamenting is encouraged and modeled in Scripture. Murmuring or complaining is not. Lamenting recognizes that God is still in charge. Complaining cops the attitude that God messed up and He is not worth bothering with anymore. When I pour out my heart to my Father, I am reminded that God's hold on me is inseparable, and nothing in heaven or earth can catch Him off guard.

Remembering God's faithfulness in the past also helps me to hold onto hope. If you were a history buff in ancient Israel then God probably chose you to be a prophet. Whenever the people wandered off into the latest idol trend, the prophets recounted God's great miracles and mercies in the nation's past. How could they forget the plagues in Egypt? Did they not remember what God did at the Red Sea? In fact, the prophets specifically rebuked the people for their forgetfulness.

When I feel that life has backed me into a corner, I must remind myself that it is not the first time, I have been here before. God has always come through for me in the past - like the summer after my high school graduation when all my closest friends moved, like the time I was mocked incessantly at work for my faith, or the time my girlfriend broke her word and broke my heart in the process. Amidst those painful events Jesus seemed nearer than ever before. God writes many episodes of deliverance into our life stories so that when the plot takes an unexpected turn, we can remember that we have been here before. He will do a new work now, as He did a new work then.

Imagination also enlarges our hope. Recently I have begun to appreciate the gift God has given us in our imaginations. For a long time I thought your imagination was something to be used in kindergarten and discarded by first grade. Now I realize that God has given us the ability to imagine because it expands our hope.

I like to think of our imaginations as the ability to peek behind the curtain of eternity. Reflecting on what could be is quite often a glance at what God wants to do. Friendship. Heaven. Victory. Romance. How can we hope for these things if we are not forming a picture of them in our hearts? Do not let anyone steal this gift from you. We can expand our hope and enlarge our desires when we imagine a great future that includes a wedding, honeymoon, and marriage. Painting such a picture in our minds will consequently invigorate our prayers because we realize that the future is out of our control. Whoever said that dreams and imaginations are only for fools must have known a different Jesus than the one I worship.

Finally, there is no better way to help us hold onto hope than persistent prayer. Fervent and continuous prayer is like Pilates for our weak desires. What a great invitation we have from Jesus Himself who told entire parables to encourage us to pray and never give up. Who could forget the widow who prayed day and night for justice and finally received it because God rewarded her persistence (Luke 18:1-8)? Her story shows how important prayer is for singles. As a result I have tried to make it a habit to nag God about my desire for a spouse. *Hey God, I would really like a wife. Hey God, what do you think about getting me married? Hey Lord, I just want to remind you that I would really like to fall in love. Jesus could you please, please send me someone soon?* I do not do this with a whiny, bitter heart, rather taking God at His word, I try to stay in constant conversation with Him. The great part is He never hangs up on me, sends me to His voicemail, or tells me to leave Him alone. Neither does He grow tired of my asking. Rather, I feel His delight and see His smile when I tell Him how much my desire for a spouse is truly on my heart. He already knows, but He blesses me every time He hears me ask. And believe me, I ask a lot.

THE JOURNEY HOME

If you told me ten years ago that I would one day write a book on being single later in life than expected, I would have said you were talking to the wrong guy. When I graduated from college I had my life all planned out. I knew where I was going. I would not be like those other people, who do not have life figured out and end up in strange places. I intended to do life the right way; I would follow the rules and be successful. After all, there is simply something wrong with people who do not get married right away.

It turns out I have become one of those other people. The journey of my life has taken some unexpected turns. Some of them I have liked and some of them I have not. All of them have come from the hand of God. I approved of God's plan to move me to Florida, give me great friends, and bless me as a writer. Yet, I did not approve of His decision to keep me single this long. Surely He messed things up. He fell asleep on the job. He did not draw my number. He misunderstood my prayers.

He forgot how He made me. He forgot my loneliness. He forgot me.

When my mind spirals out of control with these thoughts I lose sight of a very important fact: the single journey is not *the* journey. The sole purpose of my life is not to get married. Even if it was that makes for a very lackluster life. The temptation for singles who expect their wedding earlier than God's timetable is to place greater expectations on marriage than it can handle. No doubt a lifetime relationship with a loving partner is one of life's greatest joys, but to be frank I am sure it will not meet the burden of all my expectations. In fact, if I make the single journey the only journey of my life, I will place such a burden on my mate that she will crumble beneath its weight, regardless of how many ways I can count that I love her.

Sometimes it just seems like nothing is right in the world because I am not married. Everything would be better and more opportunities available if only I was married. It is so easy to pin the pain of a moment on what we believe we are missing. If I have a bad day at work, it is because God has not given me a spouse. If I am short on money, it is because I am not married. If I am late for an appointment, it is because I have no wife. If my favorite driver did not win the race today, it is because I had no spouse to cheer him on. All of this is, of course, silly thinking. We all know that marriage can bring more struggle to our lives than expected. But in my most despairing moments I cry out to God and say, "I am so sick and tired of my life! All I want to do is just get married!"

Nothing could be further from the truth. The reality is I want a whole lot more out of life than just someone to sleep

Chapter Eight - Hope

beside me. I want new and exciting friendships that grow deeper and deeper. I want to experience victory after victory from seeing God's kingdom advance. I want my mentors to call me out of my skin in grander and more glorious ways. I want God to invite me to risk new adventures for Him and trust Him along the way. I want to travel, dive, draw, write, read, explore, swim, ski, climb, hike, and discover far more than I have in the past. The truth is I want far more than just getting married. The good news is God wants so much more for me as well.

The single journey is not *the* journey. It is only one stretch of the much grander journey of our lives. The sooner we singles understand this the richer our lives will be. We are simultaneously on other journeys right now as well, the journey to grow in God's love, the journey of education, the journey of our careers, the journey of friendship, the journey of healing, and the journey to expand the reign of our Father the Great King. How boring to limit our life's quest to finding a spouse. We have been given a much more glorious invitation by Jesus' words: "Follow me."

The single journey is not *the* journey. There will be many journeys to come. For most of us someday a wedding will come and we will hopefully embark on a life long trip to discover the deep heart of our spouse. Children may be born and the journey of parenthood will commence. Loved ones will pass on and again we will have to set out on a lonely course through life without the people we deeply treasured. The journey of our last years, as well as death, will be an excursion we will try to avoid, but must face nevertheless.

The single journey is not *the* journey - it is only a breath. Just like everything else in this life, it is here for a moment and then it is gone; remaining only as a memory. Someday the temporal will give way to the eternal. Someday all journeys will end and all the travelers who are children of the Great King will be gathered to His castle. There will be no more wars, recessions, or famines to tear nations apart; no more earthquakes, cancers, or drive-by shootings to snatch the lives of the innocent; and no more tears, worries, burdens, or broken hearts even for singles. We will be home in the castle. We will never again be alone. The church will be in perfect union with her groom, Christ Jesus. Everlasting joy will be ours. The temporal journey will be over; the eternal journey will begin.

SOMEWHERE

I try to get away for a personal retreat at least twice each year. It is a break from a hectic schedule, but also my chance to run away and be with my God. I usually end up in the Keys. Summers can be oppressively hot in south Florida, so I usually show up in the spring or fall. If you visit the Keys after March, the Spring Breakers have left and the islands are all yours until the summer tourists arrive. The sun feels warm against your face, but a gentle breeze keeps the air comfortable and causes the palm fronds to gently wave as you pass by on your way to the shore. Sandy coasts can be scarce in the Keys, but one of my favorites is in Bahia Honda State Park on Big Pine Key where a flat stretch of sand elbows its way into the sea, unperturbed, as the waves gently slap its side. A platform of blue-green water stretches for miles in front of me as I make a nest on the shore.

I have come here to journal again. I guess that is what writers do. Even when we go on vacation we must pick up a pen. Something about recording my thoughts on a page helps me remember that my life is a story. I am by myself on the sand. There is nobody around. It is getting late and the park is

Chapter Eight - Hope

about to close. I will need to leave soon, but not before I record what great things I saw today, the thoughts I considered, the emotions I felt, and the dreams I conceived. My Father reminded me again today that I am His son. I wondered what my friends did today. I cannot wait to tell Larry about this trip.

And then it strikes me. I have to put the pen down and the journal to my side. Someday life will not be like this. Someday I will be with someone. Someday I will not travel alone. Someday I will walk the shore with the one to whom I pledged until death do us part - the one my Father gives me.

I stare at the sea until a park ranger startles me and tells me the park is closing. I collect my things and begin to walk off the sand, but not until I stop and look over my shoulder to share with God my heart's plea once again. As I turn and resume making tracks in the sand the strains of a song play softly in my ears. Although the words were written about a love that was lost, I join in and sing the words about a love I hope to find.

On the coast of somewhere beautiful
Trade winds blowin' through her hair
Sunlight dancin' on the water
And I wish I was there
Don't know how I'm gonna find her
All I know so far
She's on the coast of somewhere beautiful
Runnin' with my heart.
  - ("On the Coast of Somewhere Beautiful" by Kenny Chesney, *No Shoes, No Shirt, No Problems*, Copyright 2002)

The Single Journey

ABOUT THE AUTHOR

Peter Nadeau is a writer, teacher, and speaker. He received his M.A. in history from Tufts University and his M.A. in theological studies from Reformed Theological Seminary. Pete has organized and taught at several men's retreats sponsored by Braveheart Counseling in Winter Park, Florida. He has also written several Bible studies and theology guides for Ligonier Ministries in Lake Mary, Florida. He loves to live in Florida where he can pursue his passions of scuba diving, racing, jet skiing, and relaxing on the beach. *The Single Journey* is his first book.

Peter Nadeau is available for speaking engagements and personal appearances. For more information contact Peter at:

singlejourney.com

To order additional copies of this book or to see a complete list of all **ADVANTAGE BOOKS™** visit our online bookstore at:

www.advantagebookstore.com

or call our toll free order number at: 1-888-383-3110

Advantage BOOKS

Longwood, Florida, USA

"*we bring dreams to life*" ™
www.advbooks.com